GW00871205

DEFEI
OF THE
MUSLIM
LANDS

DEFENCE OF THE MUSLIM LANDS

by

Shaheed Dr Sheikh Abdullah Azzam

Second English Edition

Azzam Publications
BCM UHUD
London WC1N 3XX
UNITED KINGDOM
http://www.azzam.com
azzam@azzam.com

Published by:

Azzam Publications
BCM UHUD
London WC1N 3XX
UNITED KINGDOM
http://www.azzam.com
azzam@azzam.com

First English Edition   : August 1996
Second English Edition : September 2002

ISBN: 0-9540843-1-4

Worldwide Wholesale Enquiries:

Maktabah Al-Ansaar Islamic Booksellers and Publishers
567 Stratford Road
Birmingham B11 4LS
UNITED KINGDOM
Tel: +44-(0)121-771 1661
Fax: +44-(0)121-772 8525
http://www.maktabah.net
info@maktabah.net

CONTENTS

vi

Dedicated to Sheikh Abdullah Azzam and the Mujahideen of Afghanistan who ignited the flame of Jihad in the 20th Century and launched the vessel of this Deen upon this blessed path, raising its banner high with honour and dignity. Amongst them were those that joined the Caravans of Martyrs and amongst them are those that are still waiting…

"From amongst the believers are men who have been true to the covenant that they made with Allah (i.e. been martyred in His Way) and amongst them are those that are still waiting, but they have never changed in their determination in the least."
[Quran 33:23]

PUBLISHER'S FOREWORD

Praise be to Allah, Lord of the Worlds. The Hereafter is for the pious, and there is no enmity except towards the unjust. I bear witness that there is none worthy of worship except Allah Alone, and I bear witness that Muhammad is His Slave and Messenger. May Allah bless him, his pure Household, his noble Companions, and all those who follow them in goodness up to the Day of Judgement.

Defence of the Muslim Lands is a translation of the book *Ad-Difaa' An-Araadil-Muslimeen* written by Shaheed[1] Sheikh Abdullah Azzam in 1984, four years after the Soviet invasion of Afghanistan in December 1979. This book was the basis of a *fatwa* (legal verdict) by Sheikh Abdullah Azzam on the immediate obligation for the Muslims to come to the assistance of the Mujahideen in Afghanistan.

"Jihad today has become like a taboo subject that is discussed over tea or coffee. The one who writes or speaks about Jihad has not even spent a minute in the battlefield nor fired a single bullet in its path."

[Sheikh Abdullah Azzam]

In the world today, there are many Muslim scholars, intellectuals, leaders, academics, analysts and spokesmen who comment on the subject of Jihad in Islam. Some of them attempt to explain that Jihad was only existent during the time of the Prophet (SAWS) and now it has been abrogated. Some say that Jihad is only a spiritual struggle against one's inner desires. Some try to say that Jihad is only in self-defence and that there is no offensive Jihad. Most propagate the idea that parents' permission is required before one can participate in Jihad. Others are always seen apologising for Jihad infront of the disbelievers: in their books, interviews, articles and statements. The only thing common to those who make such statements is that the majority of them have never even spent one minute in the battlefield, let alone fight with the Mujahideen, dig trenches with them, sleep in their barracks, share their stale food, be inflicted with injuries or taste the departure of their martyrs.

---

[1] Shaheed: martyr

If one was to ask a 'Muslim' pop-star whether music is permissible or forbidden in Islam, he would go at lengths to justify his actions, bringing forward 'evidences' from the Quran and the Sunnah. However, one only has to look at the actions of this pop-star to determine whether he would give a sincere, unbiased answer. Likewise, if the scholar who has not followed in the footsteps of the Prophet (SAWS), his Companions and the early scholars, in partaking in battle, was asked to explain the rulings of Jihad in the world today, it is not difficult to guess what type of answer he would give.

For this reason, the Mujahid Sheikh Abdullah Azzam brought together verses from the Quran, authentic *ahadith* and quotes from the books of over 50 classical scholars in order to explain a number of misunderstood issues on the subject of Jihad. Amongst the issues covered in depth in this book are:

The difference between Offensive and Defensive Jihad, the former being *Fard Kifayah* and the latter being *Fard Ain*.

Opinions of the four schools of thought on the obligatory nature of Jihad.

Is parents' permission required for Jihad in this day and age?

Fighting Jihad without the presence of a Caliph or Islamic State. Marching out alone even if the rest stay behind.

Seeking help from and making peace treaties with the disbelievers.

The original translation of this book was carried out in 1995 by a group of Mujahideen in Bosnia, with a view to encouraging the English-speaking Muslims to come to the assistance of their fellow Muslims there. In 1996, a print version of this book was published with a green cover and electronic forms of this version also appeared on the Internet. However, due to the circumstances and situation facing the translators at the time, they were unable to carry out a final and thorough checking of the book and it was publicised containing spelling mistakes, grammatical mistakes and incorrect references.

We took upon ourselves the responsibility of re-publishing the book with the following modifications:

Correction of spelling and grammatical mistakes.

Correction of Arabic transliterated names.

Thorough checking and correction of references.

Compilation of over 150 footnotes.

Addition of comprehensive 'Scholars Index' in Appendix B, containing brief details of over 50 of the classical scholars whose statements and works form the basis for this book.

This book was written at a time whilst the first Soviet-Afghan Jihad was well underway, and the context in some parts may be related to this. However, since the core issues dealt with in this book are based on the texts of classical scholars, the material is applicable to all similar situations facing the Muslims.

"Indeed Allah loves those who fight in His Path in ranks, as if they were a solid wall." [Quran 61:4]

Allah loves the Mujahideen who fight in His Way and therefore it is incumbent upon the Muslims to love those who Allah loves, and not to label them with slogans of the disbelievers, such as militants, fanatics, extremists or rebels.

May Allah enable this book to be a means of clarifying the rulings of Jihad from the words of Mujahid scholars who did not fear the blame of any who blame nor the sword of the oppressor. May Allah bring benefit by means of this book, and grant us all the courage and ability to respond to His Call. May Allah not make us from those who do not benefit from this knowledge, such that it becomes a liability for us on the Day of Judgement. May He grant success and victory to all those who fight in His Way in all corners of the World. May He accept their martyrs and heal their wounded.

With special thanks to all the brothers who helped in translating, editing and typesetting this book, may Allah reward you in this Life and the Next.

Azzam Publications
September 2002[2] CE/ Rajab 1423AH[3]

---

[2] CE: Christian Era as opposed to A.D. (Anno Domini, In the Year of our Lord, referring to Prophet Jesus (SAWS)
[3] AH: Anno Hijrah, the date signifying the migration of the Prophet (SAWS) and the Companions to Madinah from Makkah in 622CE

WHO WAS ABDULLAH AZZAM?

"Sheikh Abdullah Azzam was not an individual, but an entire nation by himself. Muslim women have proven themselves incapable of giving birth to a man like him after he was killed."
[Usama bin Ladin, Al-Jazeera TV Channel Interview, 1999]

"He was responsible for reviving Jihad in the 20th Century."
[Time Magazine]

"His words were not like ordinary people's words. His words were few but rich in meaning. When you looked into his eyes, your heart would fill with Iman and the Love of Allah (SWT)."
[Mujahid Scholar from Makkah]

"There is not a Land of Jihad in the world today, nor a Mujahid fighting in Allah's Way, who is not inspired by the life, teachings and works of Sheikh Abdullah Azzam."
[Azzam Publications]

"In the 1980's, the martyred Sheikh Abdullah Azzam coined a phrase whose meaning reverberates today across the battlefields of Chechnya. The Sheikh (may Allah have Mercy upon him) described the Mujahideen who were killed in battle as joining 'The Caravan of the Martyrs.'"
[Field Commander Khattab of the Foreign Mujahideen in Chechnya]

Abdullah Yusuf Azzam was born in the village of Asba'ah Al-Hartiyeh, Jenin Province, in the occupied Sacred Land of Palestine in 1941. He was brought up in a humble house where he was taught Islam, and was fed with the love of Allah, His Messenger (SAWS), the Mujahideen fighting in the Way of Allah, the righteous people and the desire for the Hereafter.

Abdullah Azzam was a distinguished child who started propagating Islam from an early age. His peers knew him as a pious child. He showed signs of excellence during his youth. His teachers recognised this while he was still at elementary school.

Sheikh Abdullah Azzam was known for his perseverance and serious nature ever since he was a small boy. He received his early elementary and secondary education in his village, and continued his education at the agricultural Khadorri College, where he obtained a Diploma. Despite being the youngest of his colleagues, he was the most intelligent and the smartest. After he graduated from Khadorri College, he worked as a teacher in a village called Adder in South Jordan. Later he joined the Shariah College in Damascus University where he obtained a B.A. Degree in Shariah (Islamic Law) in 1966. After the Jews captured the West Bank in 1967, Sheikh Abdullah Azzam decided to migrate to Jordan because he could not live under the Jewish occupation of Palestine. The sin of the Israeli tanks rolling into the West Bank unmet by any resistance increased his determination to migrate in order to learn the skills necessary to fight.

In the late 1960's he joined the Jihad against the Israeli occupation of Palestine, from Jordan. Soon after that, he went to Egypt and graduated with a Master's Degree in Shariah from the University of Al-Azhar. In 1970, after the Jihad came to a halt by forcing the PLO forces out of Jordan, he began to lecture in the Jordanian University of Amman. In 1971, he was awarded a scholarship to the Al-Azhar University in Cairo from which he obtained a PhD Degree in the Principles of Islamic Jurisprudence (*Usool Al-Fiqh*) in 1973. During his stay in Egypt he came to know the family of Shaheed Sayyid Qutb (1906-1966).

Sheikh Abdullah Azzam spent a long time participating in the Jihad in Palestine. However, matters there were not to his liking, for those involved in the Jihad were far removed from Islam. He told of how these people used to spend the nights playing cards and listening to music, under the illusion that they were performing Jihad to liberate Palestine. Sheikh Abdullah Azzam mentioned that, out of the thousands in the settlement that he was in, the number of people who offered their Salah (Prayer) in congregation were so few that they could be counted on one hand. He tried to steer them towards Islam, but they resisted his attempts. One day he rhetorically asked one of the 'Mujahideen' what the religion behind the Palestinian revolution was, to which the man replied, quite clearly and bluntly,

"This revolution has no religion behind it."

This was the last straw. Sheikh Abdullah Azzam left Palestine, and went to Saudi Arabia to teach in the universities there.

When Sheikh Azzam realised that only by means of an organised force would the Ummah ever be able to gain victory, then Jihad and the gun became his pre-occupation and recreation.

"Jihad and the rifle alone. NO negotiations, NO conferences and NO dialogue,"

he would say. By practising what he was preaching, Sheikh Abdullah Azzam was one of the first Arabs to join the Afghan Jihad against the Communist Soviet Union.

In 1980, whilst in Saudi Arabia, Abdullah Azzam had the opportunity of meeting a delegation of Afghan Mujahideen who had come to perform the Hajj (Pilgrimage). He soon found himself attracted to their circles and wanted to know more about the Afghan Jihad. When the story of the Afghan Jihad was unfolded to him, he felt that this was the cause for which he had been searching for so long.

He thus left his teaching position at King Abdul-Aziz University in Jeddah, Saudi Arabia and went to Islamabad, Pakistan, in order to be able to participate in the Jihad and remain close to it. There he got to know the leaders of the Jihad. During the early part of his stay in Pakistan, he was appointed a lecturer in the International Islamic University in Islamabad. After a while he had to quit the University to devote his time and energy fully to the Jihad in Afghanistan.

In the early 1980's, Sheikh Abdullah Azzam came to experience the Jihad in Afghanistan. In this Jihad he found satisfaction of his longing and untold love to fight in the Path of Allah, just as Allah's Messenger (SAWS) once said,

"Standing for an hour in the ranks of battle waged for the Sake of Allah is better than standing in prayer for sixty years."[4]

Inspired by this *hadith*, Sheikh Abdullah Azzam even brought his family to Pakistan in order to be closer to the field of Jihad. Soon after, he then moved from Islamabad to Peshawar to remain on the doorstep of the field of Jihad and Martyrdom.

In Peshawar, together with his dear friend, Usama bin Ladin, Sheikh Abdullah Azzam founded the Bait-ul-Ansar (Mujahideen Services Bureau) with the aim of offering all possible assistance to the Afghan Jihad and the Mujahideen, through establishing and managing projects that supported the cause. The Bureau also received and trained volunteers pouring into Pakistan to participate in Jihad and allocated them to the front lines.

Unsurprisingly, this was not enough to satisfy Sheikh Azzam's burning desire for Jihad. That desire inspired him finally to go to the frontline. On the battlefield, the Sheikh gracefully played his destined role in that generous epic of heroism.

In Afghanistan he hardly ever settled in one place. He travelled throughout the country, visiting most of its provinces and states such as Logar, Kandahar, the Hindukush Mountains, the Valley of Panjsher, Kabul and Jalalabad. These travels allowed Sheikh Abdullah Azzam to witness first hand the heroic deeds of these ordinary people, who had sacrificed all that they possessed - including their own lives - for the Supremacy of the Deen of Islam.

In Peshawar, upon his return from these travels, Sheikh Azzam spoke about Jihad constantly. He prayed to restore the unity among the divided Mujahideen commanders and called upon those who had not yet joined the fighting to take up arms and to follow him to the Front before it would be too late.

---

[4] Reported by Ibn Adee and Ibn Asakir from Hurayrah (4/6165). Saheeh. Saheeh Al-Jaami' As Sagheer No.435

As Abdullah Azzam was greatly influenced by the Jihad in Afghanistan, similarly the Jihad was greatly influenced by him since he devoted all his time to its cause. He became the most prominent figure in the Afghan Jihad aside from the Afghan leaders. He spared no effort to promote the Afghan cause to the whole world, especially throughout the Muslim Ummah. He travelled all over the world, calling on Muslims to rally to the defence of their religion and lands. He wrote a number of books on Jihad, such as *Join the Caravan, Signs of Ar-Rahman in the Jihad of the Afghan, Defence of the Muslim Lands and Lovers of the Paradise Maidens*. Moreover, he himself participated physically in the Afghan Jihad, despite the fact that he was in his forties. He traversed Afghanistan, from North to South, East to West, in snow, through the mountains, in heat and in cold, riding donkeys and on foot. Young men with him used to tire from such exertions, but not Sheikh Abdullah Azzam.

He changed the minds of Muslims about the Jihad in Afghanistan and presented the Jihad as an Islamic cause that concerned all Muslims around the World. Due to his efforts, the Afghan Jihad became universal in which Muslims from every part of the World participated. Soon, volunteer Islamic fighters began to travel to Afghanistan from the four corners of the Earth, to fulfil their obligation of Jihad and in defence of their oppressed Muslim brothers and sisters.

The Sheikh's life revolved around a single goal, namely the establishment of Allah's Rule on Earth, this being the clear responsibility of each and every Muslim. In order to accomplish his life's noble mission of restoring the Khilafah, the Sheikh focused on Jihad (the armed struggle to establish Islam). He believed that Jihad must be carried out until the Khilafah (Islamic State) is established so the Light of Islam may shine on the whole world.

He reared his family also, in the same spirit, so that his wife, for example, engaged in orphan care and other humanitarian work in Afghanistan. He refused teaching positions at a number of universities, declaring that he would not abandon Jihad until he was either martyred in battle or assassinated. He used to reiterate that his ultimate goal was still to liberate Palestine. He was once quoted as saying,

"Never shall I leave the Land of Jihad, except in three cases. Either I shall be killed in Afghanistan. Either I shall be killed in Peshawar. Or either I shall be handcuffed and expelled from Pakistan."

Jihad in Afghanistan has made Abdullah Azzam the main pillar of the Jihad movement in the modern times. Through taking part in this Jihad, and through promoting and clarifying the obstacles which have been erected in the path of Jihad, he played a significant role in changing the minds of Muslims about Jihad and the need for it. He was a role model for the young generation that responded to the Call of Jihad. He had a great appreciation for Jihad and the need for it. Once he said,

"I feel that I am nine years old: seven-and-a-half years in the Afghan Jihad, one-and-a-half years in the Jihad in Palestine, and the rest of the years have no value."

From his pulpit Sheikh Azzam was always reiterating his conviction that

"Jihad must not be abandoned until Allah (SWT) Alone is worshipped. Jihad continues until Allah's Word is raised high. Jihad until all the oppressed peoples are freed. Jihad to protect our dignity and restore our occupied lands. Jihad is the way of everlasting glory."

History, as well as anyone who knew Sheikh Abdullah Azzam closely, all testify to his courage in speaking the truth, regardless of the consequences. On every occasion Sheikh Abdullah Azzam reminded all Muslims that,

"Muslims can never be defeated by others. We Muslims are not defeated by our enemies, but instead, we are defeated by our own selves."

He was a fine example of Islamic manners, in his piety, his devotion to Allah and his modesty in all things. He would never adulate in his relations with others. Sheikh Azzam always listened to the youth, he was dignified and did not allow fear to penetrate his brave heart. He practised continual fasting, especially the alternate daily fasting routine of Prophet Dawud (SAWS). He strongly counselled others to practise fasting on Mondays and Thursdays. The Sheikh was a man of uprightness, honesty and virtue, and was never heard to slander others or to talk unpleasantly about an individual Muslim.

Once a group of disgruntled Muslims sitting in Peshawar declared him to be a *Kafir* (disbeliever), who was squandering the wealth of the Muslims. When this news reached Sheikh Abdullah Azzam, rather than go and argue with them, he sent them some gifts. Despite these gifts, some of them continued to abuse and slander him whilst Sheikh Abdullah Azzam continued to send gifts to them. Many years on, when they realised their mistake, they would say about him:

"By Allah, we never saw anyone like Sheikh Abdullah Azzam. He would continue to send money to us even though we were swearing at him and abusing him."

As the Jihad in Afghanistan went on, he was succeeding in uniting together all the various fighting groups in the Afghan Jihad. Naturally, such a pride to Islam caused great distress to the enemies of Islam, and they plotted to eliminate him. In November, 1989, a lethal amount of TNT explosive was placed beneath the pulpit from which he delivered the Sermon every Friday. It was such a formidable quantity that if it had exploded, it would have destroyed the mosque, together with everything and everybody in it. Hundreds of Muslims would have been killed, but Allah provided protection and the bomb did not explode.

The enemies, determined to accomplish their ugly task, tried another plot in Peshawar, shortly after this in the same year. When Allah (SWT) willed that Sheikh Abdullah Azzam should leave this world to be in His Closest Company (we hope that it is so), the Sheikh departed in a glorious manner. The day was Friday, 24 November 1989 and the time was 12.30pm.

The enemies of Allah planted three bombs on a road so narrow only a single car could travel on it. It was the road Sheikh Abdullah Azzam would use to drive to the Friday Prayer. That Friday, the Sheikh, together with two of his own sons, Ibrahim and Muhammad, and with one of the sons of the late Sheikh Tameem Adnani (another hero of the Afghan Jihad), drove along the road. The car stopped at the position of the first bomb, and the Sheikh alighted to walk the remainder of the way. The enemies, lying in wait, then exploded the bomb. A loud explosion and a great thundering were heard all over the city.

People emerged from the mosque and beheld a terrible scene. Only a small fragment of the car remained. The young son Ibrahim flew 100 metres into the air; the other two youths were thrown a similar distance away and their remains were scattered among the trees and power lines. As for Sheikh Abdullah Azzam himself, his body was found resting against a wall, totally intact and not at all disfigured, except that some blood was seen seeping from his mouth.

That fateful blast indeed ended the worldly journey of Sheikh Abdullah Azzam which had been spent well in struggling, striving and fighting in the Path of Allah (SWT). It also secured for him, the real, eternal life in the Gardens of Paradise - we ask Allah that it is so -, that he will enjoy along with the illustrious company of *"...those on whom is the Grace of Allah: the Prophets, the Sincere ones, the Martyrs and the Righteous. And what an excellent Company are they."* *[Quran 4:69]*

It was in this way that this great hero and reviver of Islam departed from the arena of Jihad and from this World, never to return. He was buried in the Pabi Graveyard of the *Shuhadaa* (Martyrs) in Peshawar, where he joined hundreds of other *Shuhadaa*. May Allah accept him as a martyr and grant him the highest station in Paradise.

The struggle which he stood for continues, despite the efforts of the enemies of Islam. There is not a Land of Jihad today in the world, nor a Mujahid fighting in Allah's Way, who is not inspired by the life, teachings and works of Sheikh Abdullah Azzam (may Allah have Mercy on him, a plentiful Mercy).

We ask Allah (SWT) to accept the deeds of Sheikh Abdullah Azzam and reward him with the Highest Paradise. We ask Allah (SWT) to raise up for this Ummah more scholars of this calibre, who take their knowledge to the battlefield rather than confining it to the pages of books and the walls of mosques.

With this biography, we record the events of Islamic history in the 20th Century which took place in the decade from 1979 to 1989, and continue to happen. As Sheikh Abdullah Azzam himself once said,

"Indeed Islamic history is not written except with the blood of the Shuhadaa, except with the stories of the Shuhadaa and except with the examples of the Shuhadaa."

"They seek to extinguish the Light of Allah by their mouths. But Allah refuses except to perfect His Light, even if the disbelievers hate it. It is He who has sent His Messenger with the Guidance and the True Religion, in order that He may make it prevail over all other religions, even if the polytheists detest it." [Quran 9:32-33]

INTRODUCTION

All Praise is for Allah. We praise Him and seek His Assistance. We ask for His Forgiveness and take refuge in Him from the evil within ourselves and from the evil of our deeds. He whom Allah guides will never be diverted yet whomever He sends astray will never find His Way, and I bear witness that there is no god but Allah, Alone, He has no partners, and I bear witness that Muhammad is His Servant and Messenger. O Lord, nothing is easy except for what You make easy. And You lighten distress if You wish.

I wrote this fatwa[5] and it was originally larger than its present size. I showed it to our Great Respected Sheikh, Abdul-Aziz bin Baz[6]. I read it to him, he improved upon it, said, "it is good," and agreed with it. However, he suggested to me to shorten it and to write an introduction for it with which it should be published. Since the Sheikh was busy, it being Hajj season, he did not have the time to review it again.

Then Sheikh Bin Baz (may Allah protect him) declared in the mosque of Bin Ladin in Jeddah and in the large mosque of Riyadh that Jihad with your person today is Fard Ain (a global obligation). Then I showed this fatwa, without the six questions at the end, to the peers of Sheikh Abdullah Al-Waan, Professor Saeed Hawwa, Muhammad Najeeb Al-Mut'i, Dr. Hassan Hamid Hissan and Umar Sayyaf. I read it to them, they agreed with it and most of them signed it. Likewise, I read it to Sheikh Muhammad bin Salih bin Uthaimeen and he too signed it. I also read it to Sheikh Abdur-Razaq Afiffi, Hasan Ayub and Dr. Ahmad Al-Assal.

Then I spoke on the topic in a lecture at the General Guidance Centre of Mina during the Hajj season where there were gathered more than one hundred scholars from the entire Islamic world. I said to them:

---

[5] Fatwa:Islamic Legal verdict given by a scholar
[6] This book was written well before Sheikh Bin Baz passed away, in 1999CE

"Agreed are the Salaf[7], all people of understanding and the Muhaditheen[8] in all the ages of Islam: 'That if a piece of Muslim land the size of a hand span is infringed upon, then Jihad becomes Fard Ain (global obligation) on every Muslim male and female, where the child can march forward without the permission of its parents and the wife without the permission of the husband.'

I have decided in the presence of the Amir of the Mujahideen (Sayyaf[9]) and by my time of three years spent in the Afghan Jihad, that the Jihad in Afghanistan needs men. So whoever has an objection from you, O' scholars, then let him raise it." And there was not one objection. On the contrary, Dr. Jafar Sheikh Idris said, "O' my brother! There is no difference of opinion in this matter."

So finally, I published this fatwa. Maybe Allah will cause it to be useful for us in this World and the Next, and for all Muslims.

Dr. Abdullah Azzam

---

[7] Salaf: Pious Predecessors, referring to the first three generations after the Prophet (SAWS)
[8] Muhaditheen: Scholars of hadith
[9] Abdur-Rabb Rasool Sayyaf: this book was written before Sayyaf joined the Communist Northern Alliance and allied himself with the Americans

"The first obligation after Iman is the repulsion of the enemy aggressor who assaults the religion and the worldly affairs."

[Ibn Taymiyyah]

CHAPTER 1: DEFENCE OF THE MUSLIM LANDS – THE FIRST OBLIGATION AFTER IMAN

All Praise be to Allah, we praise Him, we seek His Refuge, and we seek His Forgiveness. We seek refuge in Him from the evil of our own selves and the evil of our deeds. Whomsoever Allah guides, there is none to send him astray and whomsoever Allah sends astray there is none to guide and I bear witness that there is no god but Allah and Muhammad is His Servant and Messenger. May His blessings be upon him, his family and Companions.

As to what follows:

Allah has chosen this religion to be a mercy for the worlds. He sent the most blessed of the messengers to be the last prophet for this religion, to bring it victory by the sword and the spear, after he had clearly expounded it with evidences and arguments. The Prophet (SAWS) said in an authentic hadith: *"I have been raised between the hands of the Hour with the sword, until Allah the Exalted is worshipped alone with no associates. He has provided sustenance from beneath the shadow of my spear and has decreed humiliation and belittlement for those who oppose my order. And whoever resembles a people, he is of them."*[1]

Allah the Exalted, in His Wisdom, established the salvation of humanity by this rule of fighting, for the Exalted said: ***"...and if Allah did not check one set of people by means of another, the earth would indeed be full of mischief. But Allah is full of bounty to the Alamin*** (mankind, jinns and all that exists)." **[Quran 2:251]** Hence, Allah the Almighty, the Majestic has bestowed this judgement as a favour upon Mankind, and made it unambiguous. In other words, the battle between Truth and Falsehood is for the reformation of Mankind, that the truth may be made dominant and good propagated. Also, that the religions and places of worship may be safeguarded. Allah the Exalted said: ***"...for had it not been that Allah checks one set of people by means of another, monasteries, churches, synagogues, and mosques, wherein the Name of Allah is mentioned much,***

---

[1] Reported by Ahmad and At-Tabarani.Saheeh.Saheeh Al-Jaami' As-Sagheer No.2828

1

would surely have been pulled down. Verily Allah will help those who help His (Cause). Truly, Allah is All Strong, All Mighty." [Quran 22:40]

This rule of defence or Jihad has occupied many pages in the Book of Allah, the Almighty, the Majestic, to make clear that the Truth must have a power to protect it. For how many times has Truth been defeated because of the neglect of its possessors, and how many falsehoods have been raised by their allies and men willing to sacrifice?

Jihad is built on two main pillars: patience, which reveals the bravery of the heart, and generosity, by which one spends one's wealth and spirit. Yet the sacrifice of one's person is the greatest generosity, as in the authentic hadith: *"Iman is patience and generosity."*[2] Ibn Taymiyyah[3] says[4]: *"The amendment of the children of Adam in their religion and worldly affairs would be not complete without bravery and generosity."* And Allah has made it clear that whoever turned away from Jihad in person, He would replace them with a people who would perform it. ***"If you march not forth, He will punish you with a painful torment and will replace you with another people, and you will not be able to harm Him at all, and Allah is able to do all things."*** [Quran 9:39]

The Prophet (SAWS) also underlined two of the most evil of faults: miserliness and cowardice. These faults lead to the corruption of the soul and deterioration of the society. In an authentic hadith : *"The most evil of what is in a man is niggardliness and cowardice."*[5]

There have passed ages when the Pious Predecessors held fast to this rule of fighting and became masters of this world and the teachers of Mankind. The Exalted said: ***"And we made from among them*** (Children of Israel), ***leaders, giving guidance under Our command, when they were patient and used to believe with certainty in Our***

---

[2] Reported by Ahmad.Saheeh.Silsilah Al-Ahadith As Saheehah No.554
[3] Ibn Taymiyyah, Sheikh-ul-Islam Taqi-ud-Deen bin Ahmad. See Appendix B, reference 1
[4] Majmu'Al-Fatawa 28/157
[5] Reported by Al-Bukhari and Abu Dawud.Saheeh.Sahheh Al-Jaami' No 3603

Ayat (proofs, evidences, verses, lessons, signs, revelations, etc..).”
[Quran 32:24]

As the Prophet (SAWS) has stated in an authentic hadith: *“The first of this Ummah was reformed with abstinence and certainty of belief, and the last of this Ummah will be destroyed by miserliness and longing.⁶”*

Unfortunately, there were generations that succeeded the Muslims who neglected the rules of Allah. They forsook their Lord, so He forsook them. They deserted His rules and so they were lost. ***“Then, there has succeeded them a posterity who have given up prayers*** (i.e. made their prayers to be lost, either by not offering them or by not offering them perfectly, or by not offering them in their proper fixed times, etc.) ***and have followed lusts. So they will be thrown in Hell.”*** **[Quran 19:59]**

They followed their desires and the evil of their deeds was made appealing to them. In an authentic hadith: *“Allah hates every selfish, arrogant, rambler in the marketplaces: a corpse by night and an ass by day, knowledgeable in worldly affairs yet ignorant of the Hereafter.”⁷*

One of the most important lost obligations is the forgotten obligation of fighting. Since it is absent from the present condition of the Muslims, they have become the scum of flood water, just as the Prophet (SAWS) said: *“A time will come when nations will call each other from all horizons in order to attack you, just as diners call each other to feast from a platter of food in front of them.”* A person asked the Prophet (SAWS), *“Would that be because of our small numbers in that time?”* The Prophet (SAWS) said, *“No, but you will be scum like the scum of flood water. Allah will put Wahn into your hearts and remove the fear from the hearts of your enemies.”* It was asked: *“And what is ‘Wahn’ O’ Messenger of Allah (SAWS)?”* He (SAWS) replied: *“Love of this life and hatred for death (in Allah’s Cause).”⁸*

---

⁶ Reported by Ahmad, At-Tabarani and Al-Baihaqi.Saheeh.Saheeh Al-Jaami No.3739
⁷ Saheeh Al-Jaami ‘As-Sagheer No.1874
⁸ Reported by Abu Dawud as Saheeh and Ahmad with a good chain, with the words ‘Hatred for fighting” Silsilah Al-Ahadith As-Saheehah No.958

Jihad Against the Disbelievers is of Two Types

Offensive Jihad (where the enemy is attacked in his own territory)

Where the disbelievers are not gathering to fight the Muslims, the fighting becomes *Fard Kifayah* with the minimum requirement of appointing believers to guard borders, and the sending of an army at least once a year to terrorise the enemies of Allah. It is a duty upon the Imam to assemble and send out an army unit into the land of war once or twice every year. Moreover, it is the responsibility of the Muslim population to assist him, and if he does not send an army he is in sin[9].

The scholars have mentioned that this type of Jihad is for maintaining the payment of Jizya[10]. The scholars of the principles of religion have also said: *"Jihad is Dawah with a force, and is obligatory to perform with all available capabilities, until there remains only Muslims or people who submit to Islam."*[11]

Defensive Jihad

This is expelling the disbelievers from our land, and it is *Fard Ain*, a compulsory duty upon all. It is the most important of the compulsory duties and arises in the following conditions:

> A) If the disbelievers enter a land of the Muslims.
> B) If the rows meet in battle and they begin to approach each other.
> C) If the Imam calls a person or a people to march forward, then they must march.
> D) If the disbelievers capture and imprison a group of Muslims.

---

[9] Hashiyah ibn Abidin 3/238

[10] Jizya:Compulsory tax paid by non-Muslim residents of an Islamic State in return for protection from external enemies and exemption from military service

[11] Hashiyah Ash-Shirwani and Ibn Al-Qasim in Tuhfah Al-Muhtaj Alal-Minhaj 9/213

The First Condition: If the Disbelievers Enter a Muslim Land

In this condition, the Salaf, those who succeeded them, the scholars of the four *Mathhabs* (Maliki, Hanafi, Shafi and Hanbali), the Muhadditheen, and the *tafseer* commentators, are agreed that in all Islamic ages, Jihad under this condition becomes *Fard Ain* upon the Muslims of the land which the disbelievers have attacked and upon the Muslims close by, where the children can march forth without the permission of the parents, the wife without the permission of her husband and the debtor without the permission of the creditor. If the Muslims of this land cannot expel the disbelievers because of a lack of forces, because they are lazy, indolent or simply do not act, then the *Fard Ain* obligation spreads in the shape of a circle from the nearest to the next nearest. If they too slacken or there is again a shortage of manpower, then it is upon the people behind them, and on the people behind them, to march forward. This process continues until it becomes *Fard Ain* upon the whole world. Sheikh Ibn Taymiyyah says on this topic:

"The Defensive Jihad, which is repelling an aggressor, is the most tasking type of Jihad. As agreed upon by everyone, it is obligatory to protect the religion and what is sacred. The first obligation after Iman is the repulsion of the enemy aggressor who assaults the religion and the worldly affairs. There are no conditional requirements such as supplies or transport, rather he is fought with all immediate capability. The scholars, our peers and others have spoken about this."

Ibn Taymiyyah supports his opinion of the absence of the requirement of transport in his reply to the Judge who said: *"If Jihad becomes Fard Ain upon the people of a country, one of the requirements, in comparison to Hajj, is that one must have supplies and transport if the distance is such that one shortens the prayer."*

Ibn Taymiyyah commented: *"What the Judge has said in comparison to Hajj has not been stated before by anybody and is a weak argument. Jihad is obligatory because it is for the repulsion of the harm of the enemy and therefore it has priority over Hajj. For Hajj, no transport is considered necessary. Of the Jihads some take priority. It is furthered in a Saheeh hadith narrated by Ibad bin Asamat that the Prophet (SAWS) said: 'It is upon the Muslim to listen and obey, in hardship and prosperity, in what he likes and dislikes, and even if he is not given*

5

his rights.' Therefore, the pillar of the most important of obligations is the marching forward in times of hardship as well as prosperity. As has been stated, contrary to Hajj, the obligation remains in times of hardship. This is in offensive Jihad, yet it is clear that defensive Jihad carries a greater degree of obligation. To defend the sacred things and the religion from the aggressor is obligatory, as agreed upon by everyone. The first obligation after Iman is repulsion of the enemy aggressor who assaults the religion and the worldly affairs"[12] Now we look at the opinions of the four Mathhabs who are all in agreement on this point.

Opinions of the Four Schools of Thought

Hanafi[13] Fiqh

Ibn Abidin[14] said[15]: *"Jihad becomes Fard Ain if the enemy attacks one of the borders of the Muslims and it becomes Fard Ain upon those close by. For those who are far away, it is Fard Kifayah, if their assistance is not required. If they are needed, perhaps because those near the attack cannot resist the enemy, or are lazy and do not fight Jihad, then it becomes Fard Ain upon those behind them, like the obligation to pray and fast. There is no room for them to leave it. If they too are unable, then it becomes Fard Ain upon those behind them, and so on in the same manner until the Jihad becomes Fard Ain upon the whole Ummah of Islam from the East to the West."*

The following have similar *fatawa*: Al-Kassani[16,17] , Ibn Najim[18,19] and Ibn Hammam [20,21].

---

[12] Kitab Al-Ikhtiyarat Al-Ilmiyyah by Ibn Taymiyyah, followed by Al-fatawa Al Kubara 4/608

[13] Abu haneefah, Numan bin Thabit. See Appendix B, Reference 2

[14] Ibn Abidin, Muhammad Amin Al-Hanafi. See Appendix B, Reference 3

[15] Hashiyah Ibn Abidin 3/238

[16] Al-Kassani, Abu Bakr bin Masood. See Appendix B, Reference 4

[17] badai As-Sana'I 7/72

[18] Ibn najim, Ibrahim Al-Misri Al-hanafi. See Appendix B, Reference 5

[19] Al-bahr Ar-Ra'iq by Ibn Najim 5/191

[20] Ibn Hammam, Al-Kamal.See Appendix B, Reference 6

[21] Fath Al-Qadir by Ibn Hammam 5/191

Maliki[22] Fiqh

In *Hashiyah Ad-Dussuqi*[23] it is stated that Jihad becomes Fard Ain upon a surprise attack by the enemy. Ad-Dussuqi said: *"Wherever this happens, Jihad immediately becomes Fard Ain upon everybody, even women, slaves and children, and they march out even if their guardians, husbands and creditors forbid them to."*[24]

Shafi[25] Fiqh

In Nihayah Al-Muhtaj by Ar-Ramli:[26] *"If they approach one of our lands and the distance between them and us becomes less than the distance permitting the shortening of prayers, then the people of that territory must defend it and it becomes Fard Ain even upon the people for whom there is usually no Jihad: the poor, the children, the slaves, the debtor and the women."*[27]

Hanbali[28] Fiqh

In Al Mughni by Ibn Qudamah[29]: *"Jihad becomes Fard Ain in three situations:*

1) If the two sides meet in battle and they approach each other.
2) If the disbelievers enter a land, Jihad becomes Fard Ain upon its people.
3) If the Imam calls a people to march forward it is obligatory upon them to march forward."[30]

---

[22] Imam Malik bin Anas bin Malik.See Appendix B, Reference 7
[23] Ad-Dussuqi, Ibrahim.See Appendix B, Reference 8
[24] Hashiyah Ad-Dussuqi 2/174
[25] Imam Ash-Shafi, Muhammad bin Idris bin Al-Abbas. See Appendix B, Reference 9
[26] Ar-Ramli, Ahmad.See Appendix B, Reference 10
[27] Nihayah Al-Muhtaj
[28] Imam Ahmad bin Muhammad bin Hanbal Ash Shaibani.See Appendix *, Reference 11
[29] Ibn Qudamah Al Maqdisi, Muwaffiq-Ud-Deen Abu Muhammad Abdullah bin Ahmad Al-Hanbali. See Appendix B, Reference 12
[30] Al-Mughni 8/354

Ibn Taymiyyah remarked: *"If the enemy enters a Muslim land, there is no doubt that it is obligatory for the closest and then the next closest to repel him, because the Muslim lands are like one land. It is obligatory to march to the territory even without the permission of parents or creditor, and narrations reported by Imam Ahmad are clear on this."*[31]

This situation is known as the General March.

Evidence for The General March and its Justification

Allah the Almighty, the Majestic, says: **"March forth, whether you are light** (being healthy, young and wealthy) **or heavy** (being ill, old and poor) **and make Jihad with your wealth and your lives in the Path of Allah. This is better for you if you but knew."** [Quran 9:41]

In a preceding verse the infliction of punishment and the replacement by a people who carry Islam, has been mentioned as a recompense for those who do not march forward. Allah does not punish except those who leave an obligation or perform forbidden acts. **"If you march not forth, he will punish you with a painful torment and will replace you by another people, and you cannot harm him at all and Allah is able to do all things."** [Quran 9:39]

Ibn Kathir[32] said: *"Allah the Exalted ordered that everybody march forward with the Messenger of Allah (SAWS) (the General March) in the expedition of Tabuk to fight the enemies of Allah, the unbelieving Romans of the People of the Book."* Al-Bukhari has written a chapter in *Saheeh Al-Bukhari* (entitled *The Chapter on the Obligation of Marching Forward and What is Required from Jihad and Intention for it*) and quoted this verse. It was a general call because it became known to the Muslims that the Romans were gathering on the borders of the Arabian Peninsula and were preparing

---

[31] Al-Fatawa Al-Kubara 4/608
[32] Ibn Kathir, Abul Fida ismail bin Abi Hafs Shihabuddin Umar bin Kathir bin Dawbin Kathir bin Zar Al-Qurashi. See Appendix B, Reference 13

8

to invade Madinah. Therefore, what is the situation if the disbelievers actually enter a Muslim land, does not the march forward become the ultimate priority? Abu Talha (RA) said about the Exalted's words: *"...light or heavy...":* *'old and young, Allah did not listen to anyone's excuse.'*[33] Hasan Al-Basri [34] said that it means: *'in hardship and in ease.'*

Ibn Taymiyyah wrote: *"If the enemy intends an attack upon the Muslims, then repelling him becomes obligatory upon the population under attack as well as the population not under attack. The Exalted has said: '...But if they seek your help in religion, it is your duty to help them...' [Quran 8:72]. Furthermore, the Prophet (SAWS) ordered the assisting of a Muslim in need. Whether or not one is a salaried soldier, and no matter what his capabilities, it is an obligation upon everybody, with their persons and wealth, little or much, riding or on foot. As it was when the enemy attacked Madinah in the Battle of the Trench, Allah allowed no one to be exempted."*[35]

Az-Zuhri[36] wrote: *"Saeed bin Al-Musayyib[37] went on a military expedition having lost one of his eyes. The people said to him: 'You are an invalid.' He replied, 'Allah has ordered the light and the heavy to march forward. Therefore, if it is not possible for me to fight, I will make your numbers seem greater by my presence and I will watch over your things.[38]'*

2 Allah the Almighty, the Majestic, says: **"...and fight the Mushrikun** (polytheists, pagans, idolaters, disbelievers in the oneness of Allah) **collectively, as they fight against you collectively. But know that Allah is with those who are Al-Muttaqun[39]." [Quran 9:36]** Ibn Al-

---

[33] Mukhtasar Ibn Kathit 2/144
[34] Hasan Al-basri. Al-Hasan bin Abil-Hasan Yasar Abu Saeed Al Basri. See Appendix B, Reference 14
[35] Majmu'Al-Fatawa 28/358
[36] Az-Zuhri, Muhammad bin Muslim bin Abdullah bin Shihab.See Appendix B, Reference 15
[37] saeed bin Al-Musayyib, Abu Muhammad.See Appendix B, Reference 16
[38] Al Jaami' li-Ahkam Al- Quran 8/150
[39] Al-Muttaqun: Means pious and righteous persons who fear Allah much (abstain from all kinds of sins and evil deeds which he has forbidden) and love Allah much (perform all kinds of deed which he has ordained)

9

Arabi[40] said: '***collectively***' means besieging them from every side and in all possible circumstances."[41]

3 Allah the Almighty, the Majestic, says: "***And fight them until there is no more Fitnah*** (disbelief and polytheism: i.e. worshipping others besides Allah) ***and the religion*** (worship***) will all be for Allah alone*** (in the whole of the world)." **[Quran 8:39]** The Fitnah means Shirk as Ibn Abbas[42] and As-Sudi[43] said: *"When the disbelievers attack and control a country, the Ummah is endangered in its religion and it becomes susceptible to doubt in its belief. Fighting then becomes an obligation to protect the religion, lives, honour and wealth."[44]*

4 He (SAWS) has said: *"There is no Hijrah[45] after the Conquest (of Makkah) but there is Jihad and the intention for it. Therefore, if you are called to march forth then march forth."[46]*

It is an obligation to march forth if the Ummah is called to do so, and in the situation of an enemy attack. The Ummah is called to march forward to protect its religion. The extent of the obligation is related to the need of the Muslims or demand of the Imam, as Ibn Hajar[47] has clarified in the explanation of this hadith:

'Al-Qurtubi[48] said: *"Anyone who is aware of the weakness of the Muslims in the face of their enemy and knows that he can reach them and assist them, it is also incumbent upon him to march forward."[49]*

---

[40] Ibn Al-Arabi, Qadi Abu Bakr Muhammad bin Abdullah Al-Ishbili.See Appendix B, reference 17
[41] Al-Jaami' li-Ahkam Al-Quran 8/150
[42] Ibn Abbas Abdullah.See Appendix B, Reference 18
[43] As-Sudi, Ismail bin Abdur-rahman.See appendix B,Reference 19
[44] Al-Qurtubi 2/253
[45] Hijrah:Migration rom one land to another land for the sake of Allah
[46] reported by Al-Bukhari
[47] Ibn Hajar Al-Asqalani, abul-fadl Shihabuddin Ahmad bin Ali bin Muhammad bin Muhammad bin Ahmad Al-Kinani Ash-Shafi. See Appendix B, Reference 20
[48] Al-Qurtubi, Muhammad bin Ahmad bin Abi Bakr Farh, Abu Abdullah Al-Ansari. See Appendix B, Reference 21
[49] Fath Al-bari 6/30

10

5 Every religion which Allah has revealed, safeguards five essential aspects: the religion, life, honour (e.g. women), the intellect and property. Consequently, there must be measures to safeguard these five aspects by any means. Therefore, Islam orders repelling the aggressor.[50] The aggressor is one who imposes himself with violence upon others, seeking their life, their wealth or their honour.

A-The aggressor against honour: even if a Muslim displays aggression against honour, it is obligatory to defend it from him by the agreement of the scholars, even if this leads to killing him. Accordingly, the scholars have stated that it is not permitted for a Muslim woman[51] to surrender or allow herself to be captured, even if she is killed, if she fears for her honour.

B- Repulsion of the aggressor who attacks property and life is obligatory, as agreed upon by the majority of the scholars, and corresponds to the consensus of the Maliki and Shafi schools of thought, even if this leads to killing a Muslim aggressor. In an authentic *hadith*, the Prophet (SAWS) said[52]: *"Whoever is killed protecting his wealth is a martyr. Whoever is killed protecting his blood is a martyr. Whoever is killed protecting his family is a martyr."*[53]

Al-Jassas[54], after coming to know of this hadith, said: *"We know of no difference of opinion, that if a man bears his sword to another man to kill him unjustly, then it is incumbent upon the Muslims to kill this aggressor."*[55]

In this situation, if the aggressor is killed he will be in the Hellfire, even if he was a Muslim. Whereas, if the defender is killed he will be a martyr. This is the ruling for a Muslim aggressor, so how will it be if

---

[50] Jaami' Al-Ahkam 8/150
[51] Women are included in the definition of the Arabic Word 'Ard'
[52] Reported by Ahmad, Abu dawud, At-Trimidhi and An-Nasa'i.Saheeh Al Jaami' As-Sagheer No.6321
[53] hashiyah Ibn Abidin 5/383, Az-Zila'I 6/110, Mawahib Al-Jaleel 6/323, Tuhfah Al-Muhtaj 4/124, Al-Iqna' 4/290, Ar-Rawdah Al-Bahiyyah 2/371, Al-Bahr Az-Zukhar 6/268
[54] Al-Jassas, Abu Bakr Ar-Razi. See Appendix B, Reference 22
[55] Ahkam Al-Quran by Al-Jassas 1/2402

11

the disbelievers invade a Muslim land, where they would oppress and assail the religion, honour, lives and property to the point of extinction? Is it not the foremost obligation upon the Muslims in this situation to repel this disbelieving aggressor, whether he be alone or a whole nation!?

6 If the disbelievers use Muslim captives as human shields infront of them in an advance to occupy a Muslim land, it remains an obligation to fight the disbelievers even if this leads to the killing of the Muslim captives.

Ibn Taymiyyah said[56]: "*If, with the disbelievers, there are pious people from the best of mankind and it is not possible to fight these disbelievers except by killing these pious people, then they are to be killed as well. The leading scholars are in agreement that if the disbelievers use Muslim captives as human shields, and there is fear for the rest of the Muslims if they are not fought, then it is permitted to shoot them, aiming at the disbelievers. One of the sayings of the scholars is that, even if we do not fear for the Muslims in general, it is permissible to shoot the Muslim captives."* And he carried on: *"The Sunnah and Ijma (concensus of scholars) agree that if the aggression of a Muslim aggressor cannot be stopped except by killing him, then he must be killed, even if his transgression is over a fraction of a dinar. This is due to the authentic hadith of the Prophet (SAWS): 'Whoever is killed protecting his wealth is a martyr.'"*

This is because the protection of the remaining Muslims from fitnah and shirk, and the protection of the religion, honour and wealth are more of a priority than a small number of Muslim captives in the hands of the disbelievers.

7 The fighting of the renegade Muslim group

Allah the Exalted has said: "***And if two parties or groups among the believers fall into fighting, then make peace between both, but if one of them rebels against the other, then fight you*** (all) ***against the one that rebels till it complies with the command of Allah; then if it complies, then make reconciliation between them justly,***

---

[56] Majmu' Al-Fatawa 28/537

12

and be equitable. Verily Allah loves those who are equitable."
[Quran 49:9]

If Allah had made it an obligation to fight the renegade Muslim group, to unify the Muslims and protect their religion, honour and wealth, then what will the ruling be for fighting the aggressing disbelieving nation? Does it not take priority?

8 The ruling for the one who wages war

The Almighty, the Majestic says: *"The recompense of those who wage war against Allah and His Messenger and do mischief in the land is only that they shall be killed or crucified, or their hands and feet be cut off from the opposite sides, or exiled from the land. That is their disgrace in this world, and a great torment is theirs in the Hereafter."* [Quran 5:33]

This is the ruling applied on the one who wages war from among the Muslims. He spreads distress and corruption in the land and he infringes upon wealth and honour. This is the ruling which the Messenger of Allah (SAWS) carried out upon the sick bedouins who turned apostate as has been reported in Al-Bukhari[57] and Muslim[58'59]. What should be the treatment of the disbelieving nation that brings calamity upon the people, their religion, their wealth and their honour? Is not the first obligation upon the Muslims to fight them?

These are some of the evidences and reasons that corroborate the ruling on the General March when the disbelievers enter a Muslim land. Verily, the repelling of the disbelieving enemy is the most important obligation after Iman, as said Ibn Taymiyyah: *"The first obligation after Iman is the repulsion of the enemy aggressor who assaults the religion and the worldly affairs."*[60]

---

[57] Al-Bukhari, Muhammad bin Ismail bin Ibrahim.See appendix B, Reference 23
[58] Imam Muslim bin Hajjaj Al-Qushairi An-Nishapuri.See Appendix B, Reference 24
[59] Al-fath Al-rabbani.Tarteeb Musnad Al-Imam Ahmad Ash-Shaibani by Ahmad Abdur Rahman al Banna 8/128
[60] Al-Fatawa Al-Kubara 6/608

13

CHAPTER 2: THE RULING OF FIGHTING IN PALESTINE AND AFGHANISTAN

"And what is wrong with you that you fight not in the Cause of Allah, and for those weak, ill-treated and oppressed among men, women, and children, whose cry is: 'Our Lord! Rescue us from this town whose people are oppressors; and raise for us from You one who will protect, and raise for us from You one who will help.'"
[Quran 4:75]

CHAPTER 2: THE RULING OF FIGHTING IN PALESTINE AND AFGHANISTAN

It has been made clear in the previous chapter that if the disbelievers infringe upon a hand span of Muslim land, Jihad becomes Fard Ain for its people and for those near by. If they fail to repel the disbelievers due to a lack of resources or due to laziness, then the obligation of Jihad spreads to those behind, and carries on spreading in this process, until the Jihad becomes Fard Ain upon the whole earth from the East to the West.

In this condition, no permission is required from the husband for the wife, the parent for the child nor the creditor for the debtor.

The sin remains on the necks of all Muslims as long as any hand span of land that was once Islamic, is in the hands of the disbelievers.

The sin is measured according to one's authority or capabilities. The sin for the scholars, leaders, and Islamic propagators, who are well known in their communities, is greater than for the ordinary civilian.

The sin upon this present generation, for not advancing towards Afghanistan, Palestine, the Philippines, Kashmir, Lebanon, Chad, Eritrea, etc, is greater than the sin inherited from the loss of the lands which have previously fallen into the possession of the disbelievers. We have to concentrate our efforts on Afghanistan and Palestine now, because they have become our foremost problems. Moreover, our occupying enemies are very deceptive and execute programs to extend their power in these regions. If we were to resolve these dilemmas, we would resolve a great deal of complications. Their protection is the protection for the whole ummah.

To Begin with Afghanistan

Whoever can, from among the Arabs, fight Jihad in Palestine, then he must start there. If he is not capable, then he must set out for Afghanistan. For the rest of the Muslims, I believe they should start their Jihad in Afghanistan. It is our opinion that we should begin with

Afghanistan before Palestine; not because Afghanistan is more important than Palestine; not at all, Palestine is the foremost Islamic problem. It is the heart of the Islamic world and it is a blessed land, but there are some reasons which make Afghanistan the starting point:

1 The battles in Afghanistan are still raging and have reached a level of intensity, the likes of which have not been witnessed in the mountain ranges of Hindu Kush, nor in recent Islamic history.

2 The Islamic flag being raised in Afghanistan is clear: *"La ilaha illallah Muhammad-ur-Rasoolullah (there is no god but Allah and Muhammad is the Messenger of Allah),"* and the aim is clear: 'to make Allah's Word uppermost.' The Second Article in the constitution of the Afghan Islamic Union is: *'The goal of this unification is to bring forth an Islamic State in Afghanistan.'* In the Third Article it states: *'Our goal is taken from the words of the Exalted: "...the Command (or the judgement) is for none but Allah..."* [Quran 12:40]. *The rule is solely for the Lord of the Worlds.'*

3 The Islamists have been the first to take control of the battles in Afghanistan. Those who lead the Jihad in Afghanistan are the sons of the Islamic Movement, the scholars and memorisers of the Quran. However, in Palestine, the leadership has been appropriated by a variety of people, of them sincere Muslims, Communists, nationalists and modernist Muslims. Together they have hoisted the banner of a secular state.

4 The situation in Afghanistan is still in the hands of the Mujahideen. They continue to refuse help from any disbelieving country, while Palestine depends completely on the Soviet Union, who withheld their help in Palestine's time of dire need. They were left to face their predicament by themselves in front of the world conspiracy. The situation has become a game in the hands of the great powers. These powers have been gambling with the land, the people and the honour of Palestine, pursuing them even into the Arab states, until their military power is exhausted.

5 There are more than 3000km of open border in Afghanistan and regions of tribes not under political influence. This forms a protective shield for the Mujahideen. However, in Palestine, the situation is entirely different. The borders are closed, their hands are bound and the eyes of the 'Muslim' authorities spy from all sides for anyone who attempts to infiltrate their borders to kill the Jews.

Imam Ash-Shafi said[61]: *"If there is a situation of different enemies where one is more threatening and more frightening than the others, the Imam should engage the more frightening and threatening. This is acceptable, even if his home is further away. The reason being; Allah willing, in this manner you prove that you are not afraid and you make an example for the others. This decision is because of necessity, being that what is permitted in times of necessity is not permitted in other times. This happened in the time of the Messenger of Allah (SAWS) when he heard that Harith Abi Dirar was gathering his forces to fight him. He (SAWS) attacked him, though there was an enemy closer to him. Furthermore, when he was informed that Khalid bin Abi Sufyan bin Shub had gathered a force, he sent Ibn Annis to kill him, thus engaging him first even though there were closer enemies."*

6 The people of Afghanistan are renowned for their strength and pride. It seems as if the Glorified and Exalted prepared the mountains and the land there especially for Jihad.

---

[61] Al-Umm 4/177

CHAPTER 3: FARD AIN AND FARD KIFAYAH

"Had it been a near gain (booty in front of them) and an easy journey, they would have followed you, but the distance (Tabuk expedition) was long for them, and they swear by Allah, 'If only we could, we would certainly have come forth with you.' They destroy their own selves, and Allah knows that they are liars."
[Quran 9:42]

CHAPTER 3: FARD AIN AND FARD KIFAYAH

Fard Ain

It is the *Fard* (obligation) that is a compulsory duty on every single Muslim to perform, like praying or fasting.

Fard Kifayah

It is the obligation that, if performed by some, the obligation falls from the rest. The meaning of *Fard Kifayah* is that if there are not enough people that respond to it, then all the people are sinful. If a sufficient amount of people respond, the obligation falls from the rest. The call for it in the beginning is like the call for establishing a *Fard Ain*, but it differs in that a *Fard Kifayah* is absolved by the performance of some of the people. However, a *Fard Ain* is not absolved by any number of people performing it. [62] That is why Fakhr Ar-Razi [63] defined *Fard Kifayah* as the obligation that is carried out without looking to the souls of the ones who perform it. [64]

Imam Ash-Shafi said: "A *Fard Kifayah* is a command directed towards everyone, seeking only a response from some." [65] The definition agreed upon by the majority of scholars, of them Ibn Hajib [66], Al-Amdi [67] and Ibn Abdus-Shakur [68], state that *Fard Kifayah* is obligatory upon everyone, but is absolved upon the performance of some. People are now arguing about the Jihad ruling, and they consider it as *Fard Kifayah*, which means it is obligatory upon everyone but is absolved when some perform it. According to this opinion, the *Fard* of Jihad in Afghanistan is *Fard Kifayah*. Rather, it is obligatory upon all the Muslims on earth until the completion of this *Fard*, which is the expulsion of the Russians and Communists from Afghanistan. The sin is suspended onto the necks of all the people until the expulsion of all the

---

[62] Al-Mughni 8/345
[63] Ar-Razi, Fakhr-ud-Deen. See Appendix B, Reference 25
[64] Al-Mahsool by Ar-Razi, verification by Dr. Taha Jabir 2/31
[65] Usool Al-Fiqh by Abi Zahrah
[66] Ibn Hajib, Uthman bin Uthman. See Appendix B, Reference 26
[67] Al-Amdi, Saifudeen. See Apendix B, Reference 27
[68] Ibn Abdus-Shakur. See Appendix B, Reference 28

Communists is complete. This is because the *Fard,* or obligation, in the condition of an attack by the disbelievers, lasts until the expulsion of the disbelievers from the Muslim land.

Some people from far away say, "Jihad in Afghanistan needs money and not men." This talk is bare of truth, because the duration of approximately six years of Russian aggression against Afghanistan, the presence of five million refugees to the outside of the country and seven million refugees inside, scattered in mountains and in the wilderness, is enough to answer this claim.

Sayyaf said: *"14 countries, the first of them the Soviet Union, followed by the Warsaw Pact and the international Communists, are unified in their attack against us, while the Muslims in the Muslim world are still arguing: 'Is Jihad in Afghanistan Fard Ain or Fard Kifayah?' So let the Muslims wait until the last man becomes martyred, then they will believe that Jihad is Fard Ain, while it is known that up to now there have already been nearly one and a half million martyrs. The Afghan people say: 'The presence of one Arab among us is more loved by us than one million dollars.'"*

Sheikh Sayyaf wrote in a call to the scholars and Islamic propagators in Jihad magazine, ninth issue:

In the Name of Allah, the Most Merciful, the Most Kind

All Praise be to Allah and may Peace and Blessings be upon the Messenger of Allah: upon his family, Companions and whoever is guided by his guidance. As to what follows:

You are aware that the Jihad in Afghanistan began and still continues, to raise the Word of Allah in order to establish a state founded on the Quran. To realise this objective we need Mujahideen who properly understand Islam and who can safeguard the principles of a true Islamic Jihad. Therefore, we need Islamic propagators and scholars, to continually teach and instruct. You should know that there have already been many tutors and scholars martyred in the fields of Jihad in Afghanistan. This is why we are in great need of men who are capable of teaching, tutoring and directing in Mujahideen schools, training camps, refugee camps and battle fronts until Allah the Exalted helps us to bring about our expected aims. We need scholars and tutors more than any other professionals or specialists. May Allah assist us and you in serving Islam and the Muslims.

Your Brother

Abdur-Rabbir-Rasool Sayyaf
Paktia, Jaji
3 Shawwal 1405AH

Permission From Parents, Husband and Creditor

The need for permission is related to the status of the enemy:

If the enemy is inside his own country, he is not gathering around the borders, there is no effect on the Muslim country and borders are full of soldiers, then Jihad in such a situation is only *Fard Kifayah*, and permission is required from the above categories of people. This is because obedience to parents and husband is *Fard Ain* and Jihad is merely *Fard Kifayah* in this case.

If the enemy attacks a Muslim border or enters any Islamic land, then as we mentioned before, Jihad becomes *Fard Ain* upon the entire population of the country and all those around it. In this situation, permission is not required from the above categories of people. There is no permission required for anyone from the other: even the child can go out without the permission of his parents, the wife without the permission of her husband and the debtor without the permission of his creditor.

The situation of the permission from parents and husband not being required is sustained until the enemy is expelled from the Muslim land, or when there is the accumulation of sufficient numbers to expel the enemy, even if this means that all the Muslims on the earth are assembled.

Jihad, when it is *Fard Ain*, takes precedence over the obedience to parents, which is also *Fard Ain*. This is because Jihad is the protection of the religion and obedience to parents is caring for the individual.

21

Therefore, Jihad (with the parents' grief and distress it may entail) is protection of the religion, which has priority over the protection of the individual. Moreover, Jihad itself is the destruction of the Mujahid's self if he is martyred, in which case the protection of the religion is assured, while it is not certain that one's parents would be distressed if one was to go for Jihad. The certain takes precedence over the uncertain.

An Example of Fard Ain and Fard Kifayah

Some people are walking along the sea shore and amongst them is a group of good swimmers. They see a child about to drown. It shouts, *"Save me!"*, but nobody moves towards him. One of the swimmers wants to move to save him but his father forbids him. Can any scholar in this day and age say that he must obey his father and let the child drown?

This is the example of Afghanistan today. She is crying out for help, her children are being slaughtered, her women are being raped, the innocent are killed and their corpses scattered, and when sincere, young men want to move to save and assist them, they are criticised and blamed: *"How could you leave without your parents' permission?"*

Saving the drowning child is *Fard* on all the swimmers who witness him. Before anyone moves there is a call for all to save him. If someone moves to save him, the sin falls from the rest, but if no-one or not enough people move, all the swimmers are in sin.

No permission is required before anyone moves. Even if the parents forbid the son to save the drowner, they must not be obeyed. This is because the call in the beginning for a *Fard Kifayah* is the same as the call for a *Fard Ain*. The difference emerges only after. If some answer the call, then the sin falls from the rest. If none respond, all are in sin.

Ibn Taymiyyah said: *"If the enemy attacks, there is no room for argument. In fact, defence of their onslaught on religion, lives and all things held dear is obligatory as agreed upon by all."*[69]

---

[69] Al-Fatawa Al-Kubra 4/607

The evidence for the permission from parents in *Fard Kifayah* and the absence of permission in *Fard Ain* is taken from the reconciliation of two hadith:

First: A *hadith reported* by Al-Bukhari. Abdullah bin Amr bin Al-Aas (RA) said: *"A man came to the Prophet (SAWS) asking his permission for Jihad. He (SAWS) asked, 'Are your parents alive?' The man answered, 'Yes.' He (SAWS) replied, 'Go and serve them, for in them is your Jihad.'"*

Second: Ibn Hibban[70] narrated from Abdullah bin Amr (RA)[71]: *"A man came to the Prophet (SAWS) and asked him about the best of deeds. He (SAWS) replied, 'Salah (the prayer).' The man asked, 'Then what?' He (SAWS) answered, 'Jihad in the Path of Allah.' The man then said, 'I have two parents.' He (SAWS) told him, 'I order you good by them.' The man replied, 'By the One who sent you with the Truth, I will fight Jihad and leave them.' He (SAWS) said, 'You know best.'"[72]*

Ibn Hajar said: *"It is understood that here (in the scenario of the second hadith), Jihad was Fard Ain, in order to reconcile the two (hadith)."[73]*

Permission From the Sheikh and Tutor

There is no narration that we know of from any of the early scholars or predecessors saying that the sheikh or tutor has the right to give permission to his pupil for acts of worship, whether they are *Fard Kifayah* or *Fard Ain*. Whoever says otherwise, let him bring forward a statement from the *Shariah* or a clear evidence. Every Muslim can set out for Jihad without asking permission from his sheikh or tutor. The permission from the Lord of the Worlds takes precedence, and He has already given His Permission. More than that, He has obligated it.

---

[70] Ibn Hibban, Abu Hatim Muhammad bin Hibban bin Ahmad bin Hibban Al-Busti. See Appendix B, Reference 29
[71] Fath al-Bari 6/105
[72] Fath al-Bari 6/106. Reported by Ibn Hibban as Saheeh and devalued by Ibn Hajar in Fath al-Bari, who said it was Hasan or Saheeh.
[73] Fath al-Bari 6/106

23

Ibn Hubairah [74] said: *"One of the plots of Satan is to raise false gods in misinterpretations to make idols worshipped besides Allah. When the truth is made evident he suggests: 'This is not the practice of our Mathhab.' Thus, remaining loyal to one he esteems and preferring him to the truth is his worship of false gods."*

Suppose a pupil wants to study engineering, medicine or history in a Western country like America, where mischief is like a black night, where temptation crashes around him like waves and the oceans of aflamed desires are astir. If this pupil leaves without the permission of his sheikh, he or any others would not be angered. However, if he goes out for guarding the frontiers or Jihad, you will find the tongues directed towards him from every side saying: *"How can he go out without permission?"* Has the sheikh forgotten the words of the Prophet (SAWS):

"One night of guard duty in the cause of Allah the Exalted is better than a thousand nights stood in prayer and days of fasting." [75]

"Guarding the frontiers for one day and one night is better than a month of fasting and praying. If the one guarding the frontier dies, his good deeds continue on after him, his sustenance is provided for, and he is safe from the fitan." [76],[77]

"A morning or afternoon expedition in the Path of Allah is better than the World and what it contains." [78]

It is upon the sheikh and his pupil to rush towards good deeds and hasten towards good, and not to let the advice of the Messenger of Allah (SAWS) escape them: *"Take opportunity of five before five: your life before your death, your health before your sickness, your spare time before you are occupied, your youth before your old age and your wealth before your poverty."* [79]

---

[74] Ibn Hubairah. Wazeer bin HubairahAl-Hanbali. See Appendix B, Reference 30

[75] Reported by Ibn Majah, At-Tabarani, Al-Baihaqi. Declared Saheeh by Al-Haakim, agreed upon by Adh-Dhahabi. Ibn Hajar said its chain of narration is Hasan. Al-Fath Ar-Rabbani 10/95.

[76] *Fitan*: trials and tribulations such as questioning in the grave or *Ad-Dajjal* (the Anti-christ)

[77] Mukhtasar Muslim No. 1075

[78] Reported by Al-Bukhari and Muslim

[79] Reported by Al-Haakim and Baihaqi. Saheeh Al-Jaami' No. 1088

24

It is also upon them to pay close attention to the authentic hadith: *"To stand one hour in the battle line in the cause of Allah is better than sixty years of night prayer."*[80] Imam Ash-Shafi said: *"The Muslims are agreed that if a Sunnah of the Prophet (SAWS) is made clear to you, it is not permitted to leave it upon the saying of anyone."*

Jihad With One's Wealth

There is no doubt that Jihad by one's life is superior to Jihad by one's wealth. Consequently, the rich in the time of the Prophet (SAWS), were not excused from participating with their lives, such as Uthman (RA) and Abdur-Rahman bin Auf (RA). This is because the purification of the soul and the evolution of the spirit is lifted to great heights in the midst of the battle. That is why the Prophet (SAWS) advised one of his Companions in these words: *"...hold onto Jihad, because it is the monasticism of Islam."*[81]

That is why, when the Prophet (SAWS) was asked: *"Is a martyr put to trial in his grave?"* He (SAWS) replied, *"The flashing of swords above his head is sufficient trial for him."*[82]

Furthermore, the Prophet (SAWS) warned about being preoccupied with the world, away from Jihad. He once pointed to a plough and said: *"It does not enter a people's homestead except that Allah enters humiliation with it."*[83]

In an authentic hadith: *"If you practised Tabaiya Al-Ainiya (i.e. selling goods to a person for a certain price and then buying them back from him for a far lesser price), followed the tails of cows, satisfied yourselves with agriculture, and abandoned Jihad, Allah will cover you with humiliation and will not remove it until you return to your religion."*[84]

---

[80] Reported by Ahmad, Al-Haakim and Ad-Darimi. Saheeh. Saheeh Al-Jaami' As-Sagheer No. 4305

[81] Reported by Ahmad. Saheeh. Saheeh Al-Jaami' As-Sagheer No. 4305

[82] Reported by An-Nasa'i. Saheeh. Saheeh Al-Jaami' As-Sagheer No. 4359

[83] Reported by Al-Bukhari. Silsilah Al-Ahadith As-Saheehah No. 10

[84] Reported by Abu Dawud. Saheeh. Silsilah Al-Ahadith As-Saheehah No. 11

Similarly, in the authentic hadith: *"Do not take Dayah[85] for it will make you satisfied with the life of this world."*[86] The Messenger of Allah (SAWS) has listed the distractions of the world and the sources of preoccupation: agriculture, trading with interest and the con of *Al-Ainiya*, livestock farming, industry and real estate. To be preoccupied with these, in the time when Islam is being subjected to confrontation in the battle field, verging on eradication, is considered *haram* and a tremendous sin according to the *Shariah*.

The Jihad by one's wealth is obligatory if the Mujahideen are in need of it. It is *Fard* upon even women's and children's wealth, even if Jihad is *Fard Kifayah*, as decided by Ibn Taymiyyah.[87] That is why it is forbidden upon the people to make savings in the time of need. Ibn Taymiyyah was asked the question: *"We have only sufficient wealth to feed the starving or to fund the Jihad, which takes priority?"* He answered, *"We give priority to the Jihad, even if the starving must lose their lives. As in the case of the human shield, in which they are inadvertently killed by our hands, here they die by Allah's action."*[88]

Al-Qurtubi said[89]: *"The scholars are in agreement that if any need befalls the Muslims, after they have paid out the Zakah, they are required to spend from their own resources to take care of that need."* Imam Malik said[90] : *"It is obligatory upon the people to pay the ransom on those taken hostage from among them, even if it exhausts their wealth. This too is agreed upon."*

The protection of the religion takes precedence over the protection of individuals and the protection of individuals takes precedence over the protection of wealth. Therefore the wealth of the rich is not more valuable than the blood of Mujahideen.

Let the rich beware and take heed of the law of Allah concerning their wealth, while the Jihad is in great need of that wealth, as is the religion

---

[85] *Dayah*: Real Estate
[86] Reported by At-Tirmidhi. Saheeh. As-Silsilah As-Saheehah No. 12
[87] Al-Fatawa Al-Kubra 4/608
[88] Al-Fatawa Al-Kubra 4/608
[89] Al-Qurtubi 2/242
[90] Al-Qurtubi 2/242

of the Muslims and their countries, which are on the brink of extinction. The wealthy are drowning in their desires, yet if only they could just abstain for one day from their desires, hold back their hands from wasting money on trivialities, and instead direct it to the Mujahideen in Afghanistan, whose feet are lacerated by the ice and who are dying from the cold. They find no food for their day nor any ammunition with which to defend their blood.

I say, if the rich were to direct what they waste in one day, to the Mujahideen in Afghanistan, their money, by the permission of Allah, would help to cause a great leap forward towards victory. The major scholars, the foremost among them, the honourable Sheikh Abdul-Aziz bin Baz, have passed a *fatwa* which declares that directing the *Zakah* to the Mujahideen is of the finest deeds and the best charity.

Summary

One: Jihad by one's person is *Fard Ain* upon every Muslim on the earth.

Two: No permission is required for one from another for Jihad and no permission is required from the parents for the child.

Three: Jihad by one's wealth is *Fard Ain* and it is *haram* to make savings while the Jihad is in need of the Muslims' wealth.

Four: Neglecting the Jihad is like abandoning fasting and praying. In fact, neglecting the Jihad is worse in these days. We quote from Ibn Rushd[91]: *"It is agreed that when Jihad becomes Fard Ain, it takes precedence over the Fard of Hajj."*

---

[91] Ibn Rushd, Abul-Waleed bin Ahmad. See Appendix B, Reference 31

CHAPTER 4: IMPORTANT QUESTIONS

Can we fulfill this fatwa in our time?

Someone might say after all this: we already know that Jihad in person today is *Fard Ain* and that Jihad is now obligatory like Prayer and Fasting. Moreover, that Jihad in person takes precedence over Prayer and Fasting, by the saying of Ibn Taymiyyah: *"The first obligation after Iman is the repulsion of the enemy aggressor who assaults the religion and the worldly affairs."*[92]

The prayer may be delayed, joined together, its rakah's (units) reduced or its movements altered when in Jihad. In the authentic *hadith*, the Prophet (SAWS) said, referring to a battle and the enemy: *"Allah filled their homes and their graves with fire as they kept us busy from our Asr prayer until the sun disappeared."*[93]

The Mujahid can break his fast in Ramadan, just like the Messenger of Allah (SAWS) broke his fast on his way to conquer Makkah, saying: *"You are going to meet your enemy in the morning. Breaking your fast makes you stronger, therefore, break your fasts."*[94]

It has been made clear to us that no permission is required for anyone from anyone when Jihad becomes *Fard Ain*, just as no permission is required from the father, the sheikh or the master, for the obligatory Fajr prayer.

Similarly, no permission is required in obligatory Jihad. For example, if the father and the son sleep in one place, and the son wants to pray *Fajr* but his father sleeps, does anyone suggest that the son must take permission from his father to pray the obligatory prayer? Suppose that the father forbids his son from performing the prayer for some reason or another, perhaps not to disturb the other people who are sleeping (who also do not pray *Fajr*) or because his father does not want to pray.

---

[92] Al-Fatawa Al-Kubra 4/608
[93] Reported by Al-Bukhari and Muslim
[94] Reported by Al-Muslim

Does the son obey his father? The answer is clear according to the following ahadith:

"Obedience is in what is right."[95]

"There is no obedience to the creation in disobedience to the Creator."[96]

"There is no obedience to one who does not obey Allah."[97]

Neglecting Jihad is a sin and there is no obedience to the creation in disobedience to the Creator.

About Permission

To clarify this question we say with the assistance of Allah (SWT), that the Companions (RA) never sought permission from the Messenger of Allah (SAWS) once the flag was raised and the *Ummah* was called forth. However, the seeking of permission and consultation from the Messenger of Allah (SAWS), was only sought if they had personally decided to voluntarily go out for Jihad or after they had registered their names for an expedition. In the authentic *hadith* reported from Muawiyah bin Jahima As-Salmi: *"Jahima came to the Prophet (SAWS) and said, 'O' Messenger of Allah (SAWS), I want to join an expedition and I came to consult you.' He (SAWS) asked, 'Do you have a mother?' He replied, 'Yes.' He (SAWS) replied, 'Stay with her, for Paradise is at her feet.'"*[98]

In another narration, Jahima said: *"I have been registered for such and such an expedition."* i.e. 'I have signed up.' This was at a time when Jihad was *Fard Kifayah.*

If Jihad had become *Fard Ain* after the call, to ask permission of the Prophet (SAWS) would be a clear sign of hypocrisy, for the decisive verses have been revealed: *"**Those who believe in Allah and the**

---

[95] Reported by Al-Bukhari and Muslim. Saheeh Al-Jaami' As-Sagheer No. 3967

[96] Reported by Ahmad and Haakim. Saheeh. Saheeh Al-Jaami' As-Sagheer No. 2323

[97] Reported by Ahmad. Saheeh. Saheeh Al-Jaami' As-Sagheer No. 7397

[98] Reported by Ahmad and Nasa'i. Saheeh. Nayl Al-Autar 8/37

Last Day do not ask your leave to be exempted from fighting with their properties and their lives, and Allah is well-acquainted with the Al-Muttaqun (pious, Allah-fearing people). It is only those who believe not in Allah and the Last Day and whose hearts are in doubt that ask your leave (to be exempted from Jihad). So in their doubts they waver." [Quran 9:44-45]

With reference to the Rightly-Guided Caliphs, Abu Bakr (RA), Umar (RA), Uthman (RA) and Ali (RA), we do not know of the Companions or Predecessors ever asking their permission for Jihad. It was not the case that every single man who wanted to join an expedition or to fight Jihad came to Abu Bakr (RA) for his permission. The important thing is that the flag must be raised and troops sent out as soon as possible.

Furthermore, with reference to the *Amirul Mumineen's* after the Caliphs, we do not know of anyone who wanted to guard the frontiers or fight in Jihad, taking authorisation from them. Neither do we know of any Muslim in Islamic history being punished by an *Amir* for participating in Jihad or an expedition without authorisation. On the contrary, authorisation was sought from the commander in the battlefield *during* the expedition or attack in order to maintain discipline and not to spoil the plan of the Muslims.

Some Muslim scholars like Al-Auza'i [99] specified that authorisation from the Imam is only for soldiers salaried by the State. Ar-Ramli said: [100] *"To join an expedition without authorisation from the Imam or his second-in-command is a hated thing, except under the following three conditions:*

1   *If seeking permission jeopardises the objectives,*
2   *If the Imam incorrectly calls off the expedition,*
3   *If one thinks he will be unjustly or incorrectly refused authorisation. Confirmed by Al-Balqini."* [101]

We point out that all this applies when Jihad is *Fard Kifayah*. However, when Jihad becomes *Fard Ain* there is no permission required. Ibn

---

[99] Al-Auza'I, Abu Umar Abdur-rahman bin Amr. See Appendix B, Reference 32
[100] Ar-Ramli, Nihayatul-Muhtaj 8/60
[101] Al-Balqini, Sirajudeen Umar. See Appendix B, Reference 33

Rushd said: "*The Imam must be obeyed, even if he is unjust, as long as he does not order a sin. Forbidding one from the Jihad which is Fard Ain, is a sin.*"[102]

We continue declaring this case: permission is required in *Fard Kifayah*, only after sufficient numbers of Mujahideen have been assembled to be able to fulfill the *Fard*. Before this sufficiency is attained, the call is directed to all and is obligatory upon all, but is absolved by the performance of some. There is no difference between *Fard Kifayah* and *Fard Ain* before the sufficiency (*Kifayah*) is met.

Before the sufficiency, there is no seeking of permission. Permission is sought only after it is known from the Muslims in the battlefield that the required numbers have been assembled to enable the fulfillment of the *Fard*.

After all this, someone may say: we know that Jihad is *Fard Ain* and there is no permission whatsoever from anyone for Jihad, yet there are still some important questions:

First Question

How can we apply the General March practically in our time?

Some people feel that the General March, as it is required in Islam, where the woman can leave without her husband's permission and the son without his father's permission, is very demanding, for the following reasons:

Any Islamic territory is not large enough for even one thousandth of all the thousands of Muslims.

This leads to the disruption of the Islamic education process which is considered to be the hope, with Allah's Permission, for saving the *Ummah*. This leads to a process of evacuation of Islamic areas, so that if everyone left for Jihad in Palestine or Afghanistan, they would leave

---

[102] Fath Al-Ali Al-Malik by Sheikh Alish 1/390

31

vacuums for the Communists, Bathists, Nationalists and Secularists to occupy their lands.

Answer:

If only the Muslims would apply their Lord's Command and implement the laws of their *Shariah* concerning the General March for just one week in Palestine, Palestine would be completely purified of the Jewish occupiers. Similarly, the situation in Afghanistan would not last long if only the *Ummah* would march forward. Moreover, there would not be an absence of Islamic Propagators, nor would their households be destroyed by the departure of their women. Instead, in every instance, we wait and we weep. We watch the Islamic region as it falls under the domination of the disbelievers, until it is swallowed whole, then we finally eulogise with much sighing and streaming tears.

Unfortunately, when we think about Islam we think nationalistically. We fail to let our vision pass beyond geographic borders that have been drawn up for us by the disbelievers. For example, the son of the town of Ar-Ramsah in Jordan, on the Syrian border, senses a belonging and thinks Islamically about the son of Aqabah in Jordan, 600km away, more than he does about the son of Dara, a Syrian town, 10km from Ar-Ramsah. This is in spite of the fact that the son of Dara and the son of Aqabah are both Muslim worshippers, but the son of Dara is more religious than the son of the Jordanian Aqabah.

Second Question

Can we fight Jihad even if we do not have an Amir?

Yes, we fight even if we do not have an *Amir*. No-one has said that the absence of a community of Muslims under an *Amir* cancels the *Fard* of Jihad. In fact, we have seen Muslims in emergency situations, at the time of the Crusades and during the Tatar invasions, fighting with different *Amir's*. In Halab (Syria) there was an *Amir*, in Damascus there was an *Amir*, and in Egypt there was more than one *Amir*. Some of these even asked help from the Christians against their brother *Amir*, as what happened when Shawar asked help from the Christians against another *Amir*, Dar Gham, in Egypt.

32

Not one of the scholars has said that such a situation and such corruption cancels the obligation of Jihad for the defence of the Muslim lands. On the contrary, it multiplies the obligation. The same thing happened in Andalusia, as the poets said:

"They were divided into sects, each in their places,
Each place an Amir and each its pulpit."

And another wrote:

"That which made me despair of Andalusia, were the kings' titles,
Great titles of which they were not worthy,
Like the cat who mimics the lion by puffing himself up."

Not one of the scholars has said that there is no Jihad under these conditions; in fact, the scholars were themselves in the front lines of Andalusia. The battle may be void of a legitimate commander appointed by the *Amir*, as it was on the Day of the Battle of Mu'tah. Khalid bin Waleed stood up and raised the flag, and by him, Allah saved the Muslim army. For this, he was commended by the Prophet (SAWS).

If maybe the Imam or the *Amir-ul-Mumineen* is not present, this does not annul the obligation of fighting and the defence of the Muslim lands. We do not wait for the Caliphate to be restored because the Caliphate will not return through abstract theories, amassed knowledge and studying. Rather, Jihad is the right way to reform the divided authorities to the ultimate authority of the Caliphate.

The Mujahideen choose their *Amir* for Jihad from amongst themselves. He organises them, unifies their efforts and makes the strong support the weak. In an authentic *hadith* from Uqbah bin Ammar, who was amongst the to-be-mentioned party, he said: *"The Prophet (SAWS) sent us out in a party and he chose from amongst us a swordsman (leader). When we returned, I have not seen the like of when the Prophet (SAWS) blamed us. He* said, 'Are you unable, that if I send a man and he fails to apply my order, to replace him with one who applies my order?'"[103]

The Messenger of Allah (SAWS) encouraged them to change the *Amir* of the party even if he was given the flag by the noble hand of the Prophet himself. How is it if there is no *Amir* from the beginning? Of the most critical situations requiring an *Amir* is that of wartime. Ibn Qudamah said[104]: "*The absence of an Imam does not postpone the Jihad, because much is lost in its postponement.*"

If the people choose an *Amir*, he must be obeyed, as mentioned in *Fath Al-Ali Al-Malik*[105]:

"*Sheikh Miyara stated that if there is an absence of an Amir, and the people are agreed to appoint a great one in this time in order to pave their ways, and to make the strong support the weak. If this Amir exerts his efforts to achieve this to the best of his ability, it is evident that to stand against him is not permitted. Whoever opposes him seeking to create sedition, disobeys Islam and disrupts the unity.*" In the hadith of the Prophet (SAWS): "*Surely there will be predicaments and predicaments so whoever wants to disrupt and divide the order of this Ummah after they have been united, kill him, whoever he is.*"[106] And: "*Whoever comes to you while you are united under one man, and wants to disrupt your unity, kill him.*"[107]

Third Question

Can we fight in Afghanistan while the leaders are separated and at difference?

It is obligatory to fight in Afghanistan with leaders that are separated and who are at difference with each other because fighting is for the defence of the Muslims against the aggression of disbelievers. There is nothing which forbids fighting against disbelievers and atheists when

---

[103] Reported by Abu Dawud and Ahmad.Declared as Saheeh by Al-Haakim and agree upon by adh-Dhahabi.Dath Ar-Rabbani 14/45
[104] Al-Mughni 8/253
[105] Fath Al-Ali Al Malik 1/389
[106] Reported by Muslim
[107] Reported by Muslim

there is more than one Islamic group present. In such a scenario, we consider the leader of each group as the *Amir* of combat for that group.

Fourth Question

Does one fight alone if the rest stay behind?

Yes, he fights alone, because Allah the Almighty the Majestic revealed these words to His Prophet (SAWS): *"Then fight (O Muhammad SAWS) in the cause of Allah, you are not tasked (held responsible) except for yourself, and incite the believers (to fight along with you); it may be that Allah will restrain the evil might of the disbelievers. And Allah is stronger in might and stronger in punishing." [Quran 4:84]*

This verse orders the Messenger (SAWS) with two obligations:

1- Fight, even if alone.
2- Incite the believers.

The Lord of Honour relates the wisdom of fighting. It is for restraining the evil might of the disbelievers because the disbelievers do not fear our presence unless we fight: *"And fight them until there is no more Fitnah (disbelief and polytheism: i.e. worshipping others besides Allah) and the religion (worship) will all be for Allah alone..." [Quran 8:30]* By neglecting fighting, *Fitnah*, which is *Shirk*, spreads, and *Kufr* (disbelief) becomes victorious. The Companions (RA) understood this verse according to its apparent meaning.

Abu Ishaq[108] said[109]: *"When a man throws himself at the Mushrikun, does he throw himself into destruction by his own hands? No, because Allah sent his Messenger (SAWS) and He said: 'Then fight (O Muhammad*

---

[108] Abu Ishaq, Ibrahim bin Muhammad bin Al-Isfara' ini.See Appendix B, Reference 34
[109] Reported by Ahmad, declared Saheeh by Al-Haakim and agreed upon by Adh-Dhahabi

SAWS) **in the cause of Allah, you are not tasked (held responsible) except for yourself...**' *What is cited here refers to spending.*"[110]

Ibn Al-Arabi said[111]: "*There may arise such a situation in which it is obligatory upon each and every one to march forward: when Jihad is Fard Ain, if the enemy invades one of our countries or he surrounds one of our territories. Then, it is obligatory upon the whole of creation to march out for Jihad. If they fail to respond, they are in sin. If the march is general, due to the enemy's occupation of a territory or its capture of Muslim prisoners, the march is obligatory upon everyone. The light, the heavy, the riding, the walking, the slave and the free man must all go out. Whoever has a father can go without his father's permission and whoever does not have a father, until Allah's religion prevails, the territory is defended, the property is protected, the enemy is humiliated and the prisoners are rescued. On this there is no disagreement.*

What does he do if the rest stay behind? He finds a prisoner and pays his ransom. He attacks by himself if he is able, and if not, he equips a warrior."

Fighting alone pleases Allah. The Prophet (SAWS) said: "*Our Lord marvels at a man who attacks in the cause of Allah while his companions are beaten back. He knows what is upon him but he returns towards the fight until his blood is spilt. Allah the Almighty, the Majestic, says to his Angels: 'Look at my slave. He returned, desiring that which is with Me and fearing that which is from Me, until his blood was spilt.*"[112]

Fifth Question

Do we fight alongside Muslims that are below acceptable levels of Islamic education?

---

[110] The meaning of 'what is cited here refers to spending' is derived from the verse *"and spend in the path of Allah"* (ie Jihad of all kinds etc) **and do not throw yourselves into destruction by your own hands...[Quran 2: 195]** for neglecting spending in the path of Allah is the destruction.Al-fath Ar-Rabbani 14/8

[111] Ahkham Al-Quran 2/954

[112] reported by Ahmad and Abu Dawud.Hasan

This question comes from certain people of whom some are sincere. They ask how we can fight with people like Afghans, amongst them truthful, amongst them the dishonest, where smoking and *Niswar* (a type of tobacco) is widespread, for which he would even sell his gun? They are a people who adamantly follow their Hanafi *Mathhab* and some of them wear talismans. Before I clarify the ruling of the *Shariah*, I say: 'Show me a Muslim people on the earth who do not have similar problems. Shall we leave the disbelievers in every Muslim land because these problems are present?'

Answer

We must fight, because fighting is based on confronting the greater harm. This principle is mentioned in *Al-Ahkam Al-Adliyyah Al-Maadah*:

Article 26: "*The private harm should be bared to protect the public from it.*"
Article 27: "*The greater harm may be resolved by the lesser harm.*"
Article 28: "*If one cannot act except by committing one of two evils, he performs the lesser to repel the greater.*"
Article 29: "*The lesser of two evils is selected first.*"

We must choose from two evils; which is the greater evil: that Russia takes Afghanistan, turns it into a disbelieving country and forbids the Quran and Islam from it? Or Jihad with a nation that has sins and errors?

Ibn Taymiyyah said:[113] "*It is from the principles of Ahlus-Sunnah wal-Jama'ah to participate in an expedition with every good and bad Muslim. As the Prophet (SAWS) informed us, 'Allah may support this religion even with a bad man or an immoral people.' If an expedition is not possible except with bad Amirs or with sinful soldiers, he must select one of the following two: to turn away from them, leaving the expedition in their hands, in which case the enemy could overrun the remaining people, which is a greater harm for them in their religion and their lives. Or, participate in an expedition with a bad Amir, and in this way the more harmful of the two options may be resolved. Even if the Muslims cannot manage to preserve all of their practices, at least they manage to preserve most of them. It is obligatory in this situation and in any similar situation. Many expeditions with the*

---

[113] Majmu' Al Fatawa 28/506

Rightly Guided Caliphs happened in this manner. The Prophet (SAWS) affirmed: 'There is good in the forelocks of horses until the Day of Resurrection as reward and booty.' As long as they are Muslims, it is obligatory to fight alongside with them."

The banner in Afghanistan is Islamic and the goal is the establishment of the religion of Allah on the earth. If only the Muslims had fought in Palestine, in spite of the corruption that was present in the early stages, and before the situation had become aggravated with the arrival of George Habash, Naif Hawatma, Father Capici and their likes, Palestine would not have been lost. On the other hand, all the leaders of the Afghan Jihad fast and pray, along with other practices, and are calling for Islam.

It is obligatory to fight with any Muslim people as long as they are Muslims. It does not matter how bad or corrupted they are as long as they are fighting the disbelievers, People of the Book or Atheists. Ash-Shawkani[114] said:[115] *"The scholars agree that it is allowed to seek help from bad or corrupted Muslims against the disbelievers."*

Sixth Question

Can we seek help from the disbelievers if we are in a weak position?

Some people believe in seeking help from America and the Western countries for the Jihad in Afghanistan and seeking help from Russia against the Jews in Palestine. This type of assistance is *haram* by the agreement of the scholars of *fiqh* and it forfeits the ultimate aim of Jihad. There are several contradictory *hadith* on this subject. The following are *hadith* that forbid seeking help from disbelievers:

The Prophet (SAWS) said to a polytheist on the Day of the Battle of Badr, *"Go back, for I will not accept the help of a disbeliever."*[116]

"We do not seek help from disbelievers against disbelievers."[117]

---

[114] Ash-Shawkani, Muhammad bin Ali. See Appendix B, References 35
[115] Nayl Al-Autar 8/44
[116] reported by Muslim, Nayl al-Autar 7/128

Then there is an authentic narration that Safwan bin Umayyah fought alongside the Prophet (SAWS) whilst he was a disbeliever. An-Nawawi said: [118] *"Safwan bin Umayyah saw the Battle of Hunain with the Prophet (SAWS) as a disbeliever."* The Messenger of Allah (SAWS) borrowed, on the Day of Hunain, shields from Safwan bin Umayyah, saying to him, *"This loan will be returned to you"* [119]

It is well narrated by the biographers that Qasman marched out with the Prophet (SAWS) on the Day of Uhud and killed three flag bearers of the polytheists. The Prophet (SAWS) said of him: *"Allah may support this religion by an evil man."*[120]

Consequently, because of the contradictory *hadiths*, the scholars differ as to how to reconcile them. The seeking of help from the disbelievers was forbidden but later abrogated. Ibn Hajar, in *Al-Talkhees*, said that this was the best reconciliation and Imam Ash-Shafi agrees.[121] The four major schools of thought are in agreement that seeking assistance from the disbelievers is restricted by conditions:

1) The rule of Islam must have the upper hand, that is to say, the Muslims must be stronger than the combined group of the disbelievers from whom they are seeking help, as well as the disbelievers they are fighting. This is in case the disbelievers decide to collaborate against the Muslims.

2) The disbelievers must have a good opinion of the Muslims and the Muslims must feel safe from their treachery. This is estimated from the behaviour of the disbelievers.

3) The Muslims must be in need of the disbelievers they ask help from

Opinions of the Mathhabs

---

[117] Reported by Ahmad and At-Tabarani
[118] Tahtheeb Al-Asma Wal-Lalghat 263
[119] Reported by Al-Haakim. Saheeh.Saheeh Al-jaami' no 3862
[120] Reported by Al-Bukhari, narrated by Abu Hurayrah
[121] Nayl Al-Autar 8/44

Hanafi Opinion

Muhammad bin Al-Hasan[122] said[123]: *"It is acceptable for the Muslims to seek help from the disbelievers against the disbelievers if the rule of Islam has the upper hand."* Al-Jassas[124] said: *"Our peers have said, 'It is acceptable to seek help in fighting, from disbelievers against disbelievers on condition that when the coalition becomes dominant, the rule of Islam is uppermost.'"*

Maliki Opinion

Ibn Al-Qasim[125] said: [126] *"It is not my opinion that the Muslims may seek their assistance in fighting alongside with them unless the disbelievers occupy servant roles, then I see no problem with this."* Imam Malik said[127]: *"It is not my opinion that the Muslims may seek help from the disbelievers against disbelievers unless they occupy servant roles."*

Shafi Opinion

Ar-Ramli said[128] *"The Imam or second-in-command may ask help from the disbelievers even if they are Ahlul-Harb (people otherwise at war with the Muslims) if he knows they have a good opinion of us, on condition that we need them to serve or fight because we are few."*

Hanbali Opinion

Ibn Qudamah said[129]: *"From Imam Ahmad, it is permissible to ask help from the disbelievers. In fact, it is Ahmad's opinion that the disbeliever has a share in*

---

[122] Muhammad bin Al-Hasam Ash-Shaibani. See Appendix B, Reference 36
[123] Sharh Kitab As-Siyar Faqarah 201
[124] Ahkam Al-Quran by Jassas
[125] Ibn Al-Qasim Al-Maliki. See Appendix B, Reference 37
[126] Al-Maduna 2/40
[127] Al-Qurtubi 8/100
[128] Nihayah Al-Muhtaj 8/58 and Takmilah Al-Majmu' 19/28
[129] Al-Mughni 8/414

the booty if he participated in the expedition under the Imam. He went outside of the opinion of the majority which does not allow him a share."

The Revelation of the Order to Fight

Many writers commit errors on the subject of the permissibility of making peace. They quote Quranic text without knowing the chronological order of the Revelation. However, they must have knowledge of the succession of verses on Jihad in the Quran that lead up to the revelation of the Verse of the Sword in Surah At-Taubah: *"...and fight against the Mushrikun* (polytheists, pagans, idolaters, disbelievers in the oneness of Allah, etc.) *collectively, as they fight against you collectively, but know that Allah is with those who are Al Muttaqun." [Quran 9:36]*

"...Then kill the Mushrikun wherever you find them, and capture them and besiege them and prepare for them each and every ambush..." [Quran 9:5] Ibn Al-Qayyim [130]explained in Zad Al-Ma'ad that Jihad became permitted during the hijrah, then it was ordered to combat those who fought them and finally it was ordered to fight the disbelievers in general.

Ibn Abidin said[131]: *Know that the order to fight was revealed in stages:*

The Prophet (SAWS) was initially ordered with *tabligh* (propagation) and turning away. The Exalted said: *"Therefore, proclaim openly (Allah's message - Islamic monotheism) that which you are commanded and turn away from the Mushrikun." [Quran 15:94]*

Then to invite with wisdom: *"Invite (mankind, O Muhammad SAWS) to the way of your Lord (i.e. Islam) with wisdom (i.e. with the divine inspiration and the Quran) and fair preaching, and argue with them in a way that is better..." [Quran 16:125]*

---

[130] Ibn Al-Qayyim. Abu Abdullah Al-Jawziyyah. See Appendix B, Reference 38

[131] Hashiyah Ibn Abidin 3/239

41

Then, permission to fight was granted: *"Permission to fight is given to those (i.e. believers against disbelievers), who are fighting them, (and) because they (believers) have been wronged, and surely, Allah is able to give them (believers) victory." [Quran 22:39]*

Then they were ordered to fight if they were attacked: *"...but if they attack you, then kill them. Such is the recompense of the disbelievers." [Quran 2:190]*

Then, they were ordered to fight with conditions, when the sacred months had passed: *"Then when the sacred months (the 1st, 7th, 11th, and 12th months of the Islamic calendar) have past, them kill the Mushrikun wherever you find them..." [Quran 9:5]*

Finally, he was ordered to fight all out in general: *"And fight in the way of Allah those who fight you, but transgress not the limits. Truly Allah likes not the transgressors." [Quran 2:190]*

This is why it is so essential to have knowledge of the sequence of the revelation. It is also necessary to clarify, that initially it is not permitted to enter into political negotiations in the stage which is for *Dawah*, before the *Dawah* is properly established with an authority that can preserve its aims. If the Islamic *Dawah* enters negotiations in the initial stage, then its agenda becomes compromised and muddled and it will become inconsistent in the people's understanding. It will have no solid foundation and the *Dawah* will be lost in political games and national ties.

The example for this period is the noble Surah: *"Say: O Al-Kafirun (disbelievers in Allah, in His Oneness, in His Angels, in His Books, in His Messengers, in the Day of Resurrection, in Al Qadar, etc.)! I worship not that which you worship, nor you worship that which I worship..." [Quran 109] and the example of the position of the believers in this period: "...Say (O Muhammad SAWS): call your (so-called) partners (of Allah) and then plot against me and give me no respite! Verily, my Wali (protector, supporter, and helper, etc.) is Allah who has revealed the book (the Quran), and He protects (supports and helps) the righteous." [Quran 7:195-196]*

42

We must proclaim our beliefs and make them heard. The callers must raise their voices until they are sacrificed on a pyre of *fitnah* in which their souls will be tried to the limit of their patience, as it was with the Prophet (SAWS) and his Companions during the Makkan period. However, once the Islamic State was established, nothing prevented them from making pacts with the disbelievers.

Conditions for Making Peace Treaties With the Disbelievers

The scholars of *fiqh* are divided as to whether or not it is permitted to make peace treaties with the disbelievers. Among them are some who permit it based on the Treaty of Hudaybiyyah. Others permit it if the Muslims are extremely weak. Others still, say that we are no longer permitted to make peace treaties with the disbelievers because they say that all pacts with the disbelievers are cancelled by the Verse of the Sword. We say, it is permitted to make peace treaties, if in the treaty there is good for the Muslims, but under the condition that there is no clause within the treaty that nullifies or corrupts it, such as:

1- It is not permitted to include a condition in the treaty that relinquishes even a hand span of Muslim land to the disbelievers. As the land of Islam belongs to nobody, therefore no-one can make negotiations over it. Such a condition nullifies the treaty because the land belongs to Allah and to Islam. It is not permitted for anyone to misuse anything in a domain that does not belong to him, or to barter the Son of Adam that does not belong to him. With reference to the Russians, it is not permitted to negotiate with them until they retreat from every hand span of Afghan territory. With the Jews in Palestine, likewise.

2- If the Jihad becomes *Fard Ain* it nullifies the peace treaty, such as when the enemy enters the Muslim lands or intends harm upon them. *Fath Ali* of Imam Malik states, on the subject of peace treaties in *Mayir* in the chapter titled Jihad: *"If the Caliph signs a peace treaty with the Christians, but the Muslims feel the only solution is Jihad, then his peace treaty is annulled and his deed rejected.*"[132] Wherever the Jihad is *Fard Ain* it is not permitted to have peace, such as when the enemy conquers Muslims. All that we have cited on that which makes Jihad *Fard Ain*, annuls the peace treaty, because it discontinues the *Fard Ain*, which is Jihad to remedy the situation. Ibn Rushd reported that the scholars are agreed that when Jihad becomes *Fard Ain*, it has more of a priority than fulfilling the *Fard* of Hajj. The reason for this being, that if Jihad is *Fard Ain*, it must be carried out immediately, whereas Hajj may be postponed. The mentioned treaty must be abandoned because it does not conform to the *Shariah*, it is not valid nor are its rules binding, according to everyone who has a true understanding of the principles of *Shariah*. Furthermore, the mentioned treaty includes the abandonment of the *Fard* Jihad. The abandonment of the *Fard* of Jihad is an illegality and every illegality is not binding.

3- Every condition which entails the abandonment of the *Shariah* of Allah or neglect of Islamic practices nullifies the treaty. It is not permitted for Russia to interfere with the government because this corrupts Jihad and its aim.

4-It is not permitted to contract a treaty including a condition that humiliates the Muslims or creates such a sentiment. As reported in a *hadith* from Az-Zuhri, who said[133] : "*When tribulations upon the people became great, the Messenger of Allah (SAWS) sent someone to Uyainah bin Husn bin Hanifa bin Badr and to Harith bin Abi Auf Al-Muzni, who were the chiefs of the tribe of Ghatafan. He offered them one third of the fruits of Madinah under the condition that they and their forces withdraw from him and his Companions. They held negotiations but did not finalise the agreement. When he wished to finalise the agreement, he sent for Saad bin Muadh and Saad bin Ubadah in order to consult with them. He explained to them the situation and said, 'As you know, the Arabs are shooting us through one bow (gathered in their attack against us). What do you think of offering them some of the fruits of Madinah?' They replied, 'O Messenger of Allah (SAWS), if you say this is your opinion, then your opinion we follow. However, we never before offered them dates except to sell them to them or if they were our guests, and that was when we were disbelievers. Now Allah has honoured us with Islam.' The Prophet (SAWS) was pleased with what they said.*"

---

[132] fath Ali 1/289

[133] I' Laa As-Sunan 12/8. Strong, with an interrupted chain of narration

44

The Ansar felt that they would be humiliated. In another narration, the Ansar replied: *"We don't give you anything but the sword."*

5- Not to contract a condition which opposes the *Shariah* of Islam. For example:

a- An agreement allowing the disbelivers to reside in the Land of the Two Holy Mosques (i.e. entire Arabian Peninsula) due to the authentic hadith of the Prophet (SAWS): *"Expel all the Jews and Christians from the Arabian Peninsula."*[134]

b- To return Muslim women to the disbelievers: ***"...Then if you know them for true believers, send them not back to the disbelievers, they are not lawful** (wives) **for the disbelievers nor are the disbelievers lawful** (husbands) **for them..." [Quran 60:10]***

As regards sending a Muslim man back to the disbelievers, there is disagreement among the scholars of *fiqh*. Some allow for them to be returned in relation to a similar condition in the Treaty of Hudaybiyyah. However, the rest of the scholars maintain that permission for this condition in the Hudaybiyyah treaty was specifically for the Messenger of Allah (SAWS), because he knew that Allah would find a way out for them. This is the majority opinion. Baraa bin Azib said: *"The Messenger of Allah (SAWS) laid down conditions on the Day of Hudaybiyyah with the disbelievers: (i) Whoever went to the disbelievers from the Prophet (SAWS) would not be sent back. (ii) Whoever came to us from them (the disbelivers) would be returned. The Prophet (SAWS) said, 'Whoever from us went to them, Allah distanced him.'"* [135]The narration in Saheeh Muslim added: *"...and whoever left them, Allah will make for them an opening and a way out."*[136]

6- Similarly, it is not permitted to contract a condition which permits the exposure of the practices of the disbelievers in the Muslim land. For example, allowing the construction of churches, monasteries or the circulation of missionaries, all create *fitnah* for the Muslims and corrupt their beliefs, most importantly in the Arabian Peninsula.

---

[134] Reported by Muslim. Al Fath Ar Rabbani 14/120
[135] Reported by Al-Bukhari and Muslim
[136] Al-Qurtubi 8/39

Therefore, agreements and the political solution in Palestine are void, void from their very origin. Any amendments are not permissible. In Afghanistan, it is permitted under conditions:

(i) Withdrawal of the Russians from all Muslim territory.

(ii) If an Islamic State is established in Afghanistan after their withdrawal, there should be no interference in the forthcoming government such as attempting to return the King or imposing practices that aim to undermine the beliefs of the Afghan people.

(iii) The withdrawal must be without conditions or restraints.

The Russians must fully acknowledge the Mujahideen and ask for peace from them: **"But if they incline to peace, you also incline to it, and (put your) trust in Allah." [Quran 8:61]** As-Sudi and Ibn Zaid said: *"If they call for a treaty, respond to them."* [137] Ibn Hajar Al-Haithami [138] said: *"A corrupt condition corrupts the contract, for example: a condition that prevents the release of prisoners, the withdrawal from captured territory, the return of any Muslim prisoners that escape from them, their settling in the Hijaz (Arabian Peninsula), the appearance of alcohol in our land, or sending back who came to us from them."* [139]

The Mujahideen must be satisfied that the Russians are sincere in asking for peace and will not deceive them. However, those who want to have peace or be its intermediaries fail to uphold the aim of the Jihad, which is the establishment of an Islamic State, because the Western countries will never accept this and in fact, they will resist and oppose it. These people fail to comprehend the aim of Jihad and they do not have a clear Islamic vision. Furthermore, it is not permitted for these people to be fighters in Jihad, which is a blessing from Allah, nor can they be its leaders. For Allah the Almighty, the Majestic said: "If Allah brings you back to a party of them (the hypocrites), and they ask your permission to go out (to fight), say: 'Never shall you go out with me, nor fight an enemy with me..'" [Quran 9:83] Al-Qurtubi said:

---

[137] Hashiyah Ash Shirwani and Ibn Al-Qasim in Tuhfah Al-Muhtaj 9/306
[138] Ibn Hajar Al-Haithami, Ahmad bin Muhammad. See Appendix B, Reference 39
[139] Al-Qurtubi 8/39

"This indicates that the accompaniment of the foolish in an expedition is not permitted. The major scholars of fiqh have stated that in the Jihad, it is not permitted for the arrogant, the pessimist, the hesitant, the coward or the hinderer to accompany the army."[140]

CONCLUSION

Finally we say that the case is not settled by long lists of quotations or the bringing forward of evidences. Rather, the matter is referred to the heart. If Allah gives it light, it will see the truth, in which everything is apparent. Otherwise, if the hearts are darkened, they will not see. *"...Verily, it is not the eyes that grow blind, but it is the hearts which are in the breasts that grow blind." [Quran 22:46]*

The vision of the heart is for evidences, and the signs of the Lord are for cultivating taqwa, obedience and enthusiasm for acts of worship. *"Verily, proofs have come to you from your Lord, so whoever sees, will do so for* (the good of) *his own self, and whosoever blinds himself, will do so to his own harm, and I* (Muhammad SAWS) *am not a watcher over you." [Quran 6:104]* This vision opens forth in the heart the springs of perception, a perception not earned by studying. Verily, it is an understanding given by Allah to His servant, for His Book and His religion according to the capacity of the heart's vision. This vision grows in the field of the heart, that it may discern truth from falsehood, the honest from the liar. The Exalted said: **"Surely! Therein is indeed a sign for the believers." [Quran 15:77]**

Mujahid[141] said: *"In At-Tirmithi, Abi Said Al-Khudri (RA) reported that the Prophet (SAWS) said: 'Fear the perception of the believer for he sees with the Light of Allah the Almighty, the Majestic.' Then he read:* **'Surely! Therein is indeed a sign for the believers.'"** **[Quran 15:77]**

Everyone who prefers the life of this world from among the scholars, he must lie concerning Allah, in his *fatawa* (legal verdicts) and rulings, in his lectures and his commands, because many of the rules of the

---

[140] Al-Qurtubi 8/218

[141] Mujahid bin Jubair Al-Makki. See Appendix B, Reference 40

Lord conflict with the desires of the people, especially those endowed with authority.

Those who serve their lusts and their desires will not be satisfied except by contradicting the Truth or rejecting a great part of it. If the scholars and those who govern, love power and pursue their desires, they will not find fulfillment unless they oppose the Truth, especially when the doubtful coincides with their lusts, thus tempting their lower nature. What is right becomes hidden and the face of Truth is covered. If the truth is evident and without doubt, he chooses the controversial and excuses himself by saying that he will find an exit in repentance.

About those, and those like them, the Exalted said: ***"Then, there has succeeded a posterity who have given up prayers*** (*i.e. made their prayers to be lost, either by not offering them or by not offering them perfectly or by not offering them in their proper fixed times. etc.*) ***and have followed lusts..."*** **[Quran 19:59]** *The Exalted also said about them:* **"Then after them succeeded them an** (*evil*) **generation, which inherited the Book, but they chose** (*for themselves*) **the good of this low life** (*evil pleasures of this world*) **saying** (*as an excuse*): (*Everything*) **will be forgiven to us. And if** (*again*) **the offer of the like** (*evil pleasures of this world*) **came their way, they would** (*again*) **seize them** (*would commit those sins*). **Was not the Covenant of the Book taken from them that they would not say about Allah anything but the truth? And they studied what is in it** (*the Book*). **And the home of the Hereafter is better for those who are Al-Muttaqun. Do not you then understand?"** **[Quran 7:169]**

To follow vain desires blinds the eye of the heart until it can no longer differentiate between *Sunnah* and *Bidah*, or it inevitably reverses them such that it perceives the *Bidah* as *Sunnah*. This is the plague that the scholars suffer when they prefer the life of this world, pursue lusts and follow after rulers.[142] The following verses refer to them: **"And recite** (*O Muhammad SAWS*) **to them the story of him to whom we gave our Ayat** (*proofs evidences lessons signs revelations, etc.*) **but he threw them away, so Satan followed him up, and he became of those who went astray. And had We willed, we would surely have elevated him therewith. but he clung to the earth and followed his own**

---

[142] Al-Fawaaid: 113-114

vain desire. So his description is the description of a dog: if you drive him away, he lolls his tongue out, or if you leave him alone he (still) lolls his tongue out..." [Quran 7:175-176]

Quotations will not suffice, because the perception of the truth relies on the enlightenment of the heart. When the heart has a strong attachment to the life of this world and the bearer of this heart is immersed in sin, *ran* (black covering) overcomes the heart, because every sin is a black stain on the heart. These black stains accumulate until the *ran* is total and prevents the penetration of light to the heart. When the heart is darkened, things no longer appear as they truly are, for Truth is confused and its face no longer apparent. The heart is inverted and sees Truth as Falsehood and Falsehood as Truth.

There must be *taqwa* so that the capacity for discernment is developed, the heart cleansed, and so it may accord things their proper order: "*O you who believe! If you obey and fear Allah, He will grant you Furqan (a criterion to judge between right and wrong or Makhraj, i.e. making a way for you to get out from every difficulty), and will expiate for you your sins, and forgive you, and Allah is the owner of the great bounty.*" [Quran 8:29]

Whenever the scholars of the past were in confusion over difficult questions they would say, *"Ask the people of the battle fronts because they are the nearest to Allah."* They asked Ahmad bin Hanbal: *"Who do we ask after you?"* He replied, *"Ask Abu Bakr Al-Waraq, for he possesses taqwa as it ought to be, and I hope he will be successful in answering."*

An authentic hadith of the Prophet (SAWS) states: *"Amongst nations before you there have been inspired people (who were not prophets), and if there was to be one in my Ummah, then indeed it would have been Umar (RA)."*[143] and Umar was true to this.

Another authentic *hadith* narrated by Aisha (RA), who said: *"The Messenger of Allah (SAWS) would open his prayer when he stood at night with: 'O' Lord of Jibreel and Mikaeel, Originator of the heavens and the earth, Knower of the unseen and the seen, You judge between Your slaves in that in which they are*

---

[143] Reported by Al-Bukhari and Muslim

49

at difference. Guide me from that in which they differ to the truth by Your Leave. You guide whom You will to the Straight Path. "[144]

Finally, we supplicate by the blessed verse: ***"...O Lord! Judge between us and our people in truth, for you are the best of those who give judgment." [Quran 7:89]*** *We repeat the supplication of the Messenger of Allah (SAWS) as reported in Saheeh Muslim:*

'O Allah guide us from that in which they differ to the truth by Your Permission. You guide whom You will to the Straight Path. Our Lord forgive us and our brethren who preceded us in faith and put not in our hearts any hatred towards those who have believed. Our Lord, You are indeed full of Kindness, Most Merciful.

O Allah make us live in contentment and die as martyrs and gather us among the group of Mustafa (SAWS). Glory be to you O Allah and Praise, I bear witness that there is no god but You. I seek Your forgiveness and to You I repent.'

---

[144] Reported by Muslim

APPENDIX A: LETTERS OF AGREEMENT

Letter from Sheikh Muhammad Najeeb Al-Mut'i

All Praise be to Allah and may His peace and blessings be upon His Messenger, upon his family, Companions and whoever follows them in righteousness until the Day of Judgement.

Jihad in Allah's cause is to achieve martyrdom, about which Allah has given the good news of their election with his blessed words, *" ...and that He may take martyrs from among you..." [Quran 3:140].* It is a progression from one abode to another, from a problematic, deceptive and unjust life to a life of happiness and pleasure.

On this topic, the generous, the Mujahid, the courageous, the wise Dr. Abdullah Azzam has written, calling to Jihad. He has explained and showed the right agenda providing sufficient evidence from *fiqh, hadith* and *tafseer.* He has revised and discussed with proofs, causing throat swelling distress in the opposition and a splinter in the eyes of the cowards and hypocrites. I say on this topic a few words of *Dawah* to the path from which there are no other paths, in this critical moment, to remove the cancer from the *Ummah* and to defend the faith. It is the whole point of this life, that it is lived in the Path of Allah and His Prophet (SAW) and His Book. That His *Ummah* may be raised and honoured and perpetuated. The believer fights Jihad for Allah such that: if he falls, he learns and if he is injured, he is forgiven for his sins. If he is exiled, he is a traveller; if he is imprisoned, it is time for him for worship. If he lives, he will become a leader; if he dies, he is a martyr and for him is good and more.

And peace be upon the ones who listen to the call and respond *("March forward light and heavy and make Jihad in the Path of Allah with your lives and your possessions. That is better for you if only you knew." [Quran 9:41])* with the mercy and blessing of Allah.

Muhammad Najeeb Al-Mut'i
Servant of the Sunnah with the most original chain
Author of Takmilah Al-Majmu' Sharh-ul-Muhathab

51

Member of the Egyptian Writers Union

Letter from Professor Sheikh Saeed Hawwa

After hearing this letter from our Sheikh, Dr. Abdullah Azzam, I consider this fatwa to be the truth and to it I call the people.

Saeed Hawwa

Letter from Sheikh Umar Sayyaf

All Praise be to Allah and may His blessings be upon Muhammad, his family, Companions and whoever follows them in righteousness until the Day of Judgement. As to what follows:

This great *fatwa* and its advice in the rules of Jihad and of when Jihad becomes *Fard Ain* was showed to me by my brother in Islam, the Sheikh, the righteous, the truthful, the Mujahid Dr. Abdullah Azzam. I read all of it and saw it to be the correct view, the truth from which there can be no divergence, and that there is no room for anyone who has an atom of *Iman* in his heart but to accept these evidences from the Book of Allah, the *Sunnah* of the Prophet (SAWS), and the consensus of the *Ulama*. I say it must be propagated and haste must be carried out in marching forward and fulfilling this *Fard* without hesitation, otherwise one would fall into the description given by Allah: *"...But when a decisive Surah (explaining a commandment) is sent down, and fighting (Jihad) is mentioned (i.e. ordained) therein, you will see those in whose hearts is a disease (of hypocrisy) looking at you with a look of one fainting to death." [Quran 47:20]*

May Allah reward the Sheikh Abdullah, for his intention and his enlightenment. May Allah help us to follow His Good Pleasure and the truth that Jihad now is Fard Ain and that there is no excuse for anybody.

Umar Sayyaf
Grand Chair of the Ulama, Sanaa, Yemen

Letter from Sheikh Abdullah Nassah Al-Waan

All Praise be to the Lord of the Worlds, and may His peace and blessings be upon Muhammad, upon his family and his Companions who carried the flag of Jihad throughout the world, and on those who invite to the truth and on the callers to good until the Last Day.

The Sheikh, Dr. Abdullah Azzam, may Allah protect him, showed me what he had written about the rules of Jihad today pertaining to Afghanistan, Palestine and other countries of the Muslims. I say, and with Allah's help:

Wherever he went he declared this *fatwa*, quoting from the schools of thought and the Salaf, what is correct and true, that when any Islamic country is occupied by the disbelievers, as decided by the people of understanding, then fighting becomes *Fard Ain* upon its people. Consequently, the wife can go forward without the permission of her husband, and the child without the permission of its parents. Furthermore, Jihad will remain Fard Ain upon every country close by until sufficient forces are attained to liberate the Muslim countries from the grip of the disbelievers. If the disbelievers are not beaten back, then, the *Fard Ain* of Jihad spreads in the shape of a circle. The nearest to the next in nearness. Until, the Jihad becomes *Fard Ain* upon the whole earth, the enemy is completely destroyed and expelled from the Muslim land. Now in this time we find many Muslims in all Muslim countries: lazy, ill-equipped and idle. So in truth, for Afghanistan and Palestine as well as other countries of the Muslims, Jihad has today become *Fard Ain* on everyone until sufficient manpower and money are collected.

Therefore, it is incumbent upon every Muslim today, capable of carrying a weapon, to march forward to Jihad to aid his Muslim brothers in Afghanistan and in every place in need, even though his or her parents do not permit it, until sufficient forces are attained and Allah knows best.

Abdullah Nassah Al-Waan
University of King Fahd bin Abdul Aziz, Jeddah, Arabian Peninsula

APPENDIX B: SCHOLARS INDEX

1. Ibn Taymiyyah, Sheikh-ul-Islam Taqi-ud-Deen bin Ahmad. He was one of the greatest scholars that Islam has produced. He was a man of vast knowledge, well-known for his expertise in all the Islamic sciences. He dedicated his life to upholding the *Sunnah* of the Prophet (SAWS) and cleansing Islam of all the deviations that had crept into it. His uncompromising stance in defending Islam against all kinds of corruption and speaking out against the innovators, caused him to undergo many trials, such as repeatedly being imprisoned. Not only was he a man whom Allah had blessed with knowledge, but he was of those who fought against the enemies of Islam on the battlefield. He wrote a large number of books (running into hundreds) on many different subjects spanning *aqeedah, tafseer, fiqh* and *hadith*. His *fatawa* (legal rulings) consist of 38 volumes. He died in the year 728AH/1330CE, in prison, at the age of 67, may Allah have Mercy on him.

2. Abu Haneefah, Numan bin Thabit. Lived 80-150AH/707-767CE, he was known as the *'Father of all the Scholars'*. He met many of the Companions of the Prophet (SAWS), including Anas bin Malik (RA) at a young age. The Hanafi school of thought is ascribed to him.

3. Ibn Abidin, Muhammad Amin Al-Hanafi. Died 670AH/1252CE, a Hanafi jurist from Damascus and one of the most well-known commentators on Islamic Law.

4. Al-Kassani, Abu Bakr bin Masood. Died 578AH/1160CE, a Hanafi jurist and author of *Badai As-Sana'i*.

5. Ibn Najim, Ibrahim Al-Misri Al-Hanafi. Died 970AH/1563CE. Author of many books, including Al-*Ashbah Wan-Nadha'ir*.

6. Ibn Hammam, Al-Kamal. Died 681AH/1263CE, a famous Hanafi jurist and the author of *Fath Al-Qadir*.

7. Imam Malik bin Anas bin Malik. Died 179AH/795CE, upon whose verdicts the Maliki school of *fiqh* was founded, the leader of the *hadith* scholars of Madinah in his time. Besides *Al-Muwatta*, a collection of *hadith* that also contains the words of *Sahabah* (Companions) and *Tabi'een* (Successors), and forms the basis of the *fiqh* he developed, his writings include a work on the Quran: *Tafseer Ghareeb Al-Quran*.

8. Ad-Dussuqi, Ibrahim. Lived 644-687AH/1246-1288CE, famous Maliki jurist and author of *Hashiyah Ad-Dussuqi*.

9. Imam Ash-Shafi, Muhammad bin Idris bin Al-Abbas. Lived 150-204AH/767-819CE. Founder of the Shafi school of thought, he was born in Syria, brought up and educated in Makkah, studied fiqh with Imam Malik in Madinah and Imam Muhammad in Iraq, and settled in Egypt in 199AH/814CE. His Risaalah is an exposition of the basic principles upon which judgements are built and underlines the importance of hadith in *fiqh*, while Al-Umm incorporates his legal views in detail. Among his books, there is one mentioned under the title Ahkam Al-Quran.

10. Ar-Ramli, Ahmad. A famous Shafi jurist, author of *Nihayah Al-Muhtaj*. He died in 1014AH/1596CE.

11. Imam Ahmad bin Muhammad bin Hanbal Ash-Shaibani. Lived 164-241AH/781-855CE. Founder of the Hanbali school of thought. Born in Marwa and brought up in Baghdad, he devoted himself to the study and collection of *hadith* since 179AH/795CE. He was said to have memorised more than one million hadith. His *Musnad* is one of the greatest collection of *hadith* containing more than 30,000 *hadith* and reports. His work on the Quran includes a book on *tafseer* and another on *Al-Naasikh Wal-Mansookh*.

12. Ibn Qudamah Al-Maqdisi, Muwaffiq-ud-Deen Abu Muhammad Abdullah bin Ahmad Al-Hanbali. A major *faqih* (jurist) of the Hanbali school of thought, from Jerusalem. He died in 720AH/1302CE.

13. Ibn Kathir, Abul-Fida Ismail bin Abi Hafs Shihabuddin Umar bin Kathir bin Daw bin Kathir bin Zar Al-Qurashi. He was born in 701AH/1283CE near Busra, Syria. His father died when he was only four years old and was taken in by his brother and moved to Damascus in 706AH. Here, he learned from great scholars such as Ibn Asakir and the great Ibn Taymiyyah, who was extremely close to him. He also studied under various other sheikhs who gave him permission in *fiqh* and *hadith*. He made many academic contributions to Islamic sciences. Amongst his famous books are Tafseer Ibn Kathir and Al-Bidayah Wan-Nihayah. Ibn Kathir died on Thursday, the 26th of Sha'ban in 774AH/1356CE.

14. Hasan Al-Basri, Al-Hasan bin Abil-Hasan Yasar Abu Saeed Al-Basri. Died 110AH/730CE. The great *faqih* and Imam of Basra, leader of the ascetics and scholars of his time, one of the greatest Tabi'een. The son of a freedwoman of the wife of the Prophet (SAWS), Umm Salamah, and a freedman of Zaid bin Thabit, the stepson of the Prophet (SAWS). Umm Salamah nursed him. His mother took him as

a child to Umar (RA) who supplicated for him with the words: *"O Allah! Make him wise in the Religion and beloved to people."*

15. Az-Zuhri, Muhammad bin Muslim bin Abdullah bin Shihab. Lived 51-125AH/671-742CE, a man of extraordinary memory and the most outstanding scholar of *hadith* among the *Tabi'een* (Successors), he was the first to compile hadith. He also wrote a book on the life of the Prophet (SAWS).

16. Saeed bin Al-Musayyib, Abu Muhammad. Died 94AH/712CE, a great scholar of *hadith, fiqh* and the *Quran*. He was hailed as the leader of the Successors (Sayyid At-Tabi'een).

17. Ibn Al-Arabi, Qadi Abu Bakr Muhammad bin Abdullah Al-Ishbili. Died in 543AH/1148CE, the Maliki author of *Ahkam Al-Quran* and several other books.

18. Ibn Abbas, Abdullah. Died 68AH/687CE, one of the foremost Companions of the Prophet (SAWS) and one of the most eminent scholars of the Quran amongst the Companions. He was known as the *Mufassir Al-Quran* (commentator of the Quran) and he was the fourth most prolific narrator of *hadith* as well as an established *faqih*. His comments on the Quran form part of all the commentaries on the Quran.

19. As-Sudi, Ismail bin Abdur-Rahman. Died 127AH/744CE, he was a reliable narrator of traditions.

20. Ibn Hajar Al-Asqalani, Abul-Fadl Shihabuddin Ahmad bin Ali bin Muhammad bin Muhammad bin Ahmad Al-Kinani Ash-Shafi. Born in Egypt in 773AH/1355CE, he memorised the Quran at the age of nine. He travelled throughout Hijaz, Sham, Egypt and Iraq in pursuit of knowledge, studying under many prominent scholars. He authored more than 150 books —most of them being in the studies of *hadith*— which flourished during his lifetime, and the kings and princes exchanged them as gifts. His book most worthy of mentioning is Fath Al-Bari, the commentary of Saheeh Al-Bukhari, which he compiled over a period of 30 years. He died after the Isha prayer on Saturday 8th Dhul-Hijjah, 852AH/1434CE.

21. Al-Qurtubi, Muhammad bin Ahmad bin Abi Bakr Farh, Abu Abdullah Al-Ansari of Cordoba, Spain: a Maliki scholar and *hadith* scholar, one of the greatest Imams of tafseer, an ascetic who divided his days between writing and worship. His *tafseer* is *Al-Jaami' Li-Ahkam Al-Quran* in 20 volumes. He travelled to the East and settled in Minya Abil-Khusayb in Upper Egypt where he died in 671AH/1273CE.

22. Al-Jassas, Abu Bakr Ar-Razi. Died 370AH/984CE, he was a distinguished Hanafi jurist and the author of *Ahkam Al-Quran*. The deduction of juristic injunctions and rulings from the Noble Quran is the subject of this book. Instead of explaining verses in serial continuity, he has taken up the juristic details as called for by verses which consist of juristic injunctions.

23. Al-Bukhari, Muhammad bin Ismail bin Ibrahim bin Al-Mughira bin Bardizbah Al-Ju'fi. Lived 194-256AH/809-870CE. Born in 194AH/809CE in Bukhara, which is in modern-day Uzbekistan, he was the most outstanding compiler of *hadith*. His *Saheeh Al-Bukhari*, the most authentic collection of *hadith*, contains 2602 *ahadith* and is considered the most authentic book after the Quran.

24. Muslim bin Al-Hajjaj Al-Qushairi An-Nishapuri. Born in 204AH/819CE in the city of Nishapur near the city of Mashhad in modern day Iran. Muslim is considered second only to Al-Bukhari in the science of the methodology of *hadith*. Muslim compiled the *hadith* book *Al-Musnad As-Saheeh*, which became known as *Saheeh Muslim*. This book, which is considered by the Muslim scholars as the second most authentic *hadith* book after Saheeh Al-Bukhari, contains 9200 *hadith*. Imam Muslim died at his birthplace in Rajab, 261 AH/876CE.

25. Ar-Razi, Fakhr-ud-Deen. Lived 476-537AH/1149-1210CE, a commentator of the Quran and the author of *Mafatih Al-Ghaib*.

26. Ibn Al-Hajib, Uthman bin Uthman. Died 646AH/1249CE, a Maliki *faqih* (jurist) who wrote *Mukhtassar Al-Muntaha Fil-Usool*.

27. Al-Amdi, Saifudeen. Died 631AH/1233CE, he was a reputable Shafi jurist and the author of *Kitab Al-Ahkam fi Usool Al-Ahkam fi Usool Al-Fiqh*.

28. Ibn Abdus-Shukur, a reputable jurist and authority on *Usool Al-Fiqh*, who died in the 7th Century AH/ 13th Century CE.

29. Ibn Hibban, Abu Hatim Muhammad bin Hibban bin Ahmad bin Hibban Al-Busti, was born in Bust, in Sijistan. He was one of the celebrities in the knowledge of *hadith*. A pious, learned *faqih*, he was one of the students of Ibn Khuzaimah. He died in Samarqand, Uzbekistan, in 354AH/967CE, in his eighties.

30. Ibn Hubairah, Wazeer bin Hubairah Al-Hanbali. A Hanbali scholar and author of *Al-Isfaah*.

30. Ibn Rushd, Abul-Walid Muhammad bin Ahmad. Lived 453-521AH/1058-1126CE, a Maliki jurist and judge, Imam of the Great Mosque of Cordoba, Spain. Author of *Al-Muqaddamat*.

32. Al-Auza'i, Abu Umar Abdur-Rahman bin Amr. Lived 88-157AH/707-774CE, he was the leader of the people of Syria in *hadith* as well as *fiqh*. He lived and died in Beirut. He compiled a book on *hadith* and his *fiqh* dominated in Spain up to the time of Al-Hakam bin Hisham (died 207AH/822CE).

33. Al-Balqini, Sirajudeen Umar. Died 805AH/1400CE. One of the great scholars who taught at Al-Azhar University during the reign of the Mamluks. He was the author of *Mahasin Al-Istilah* and a commentary on *Sunan At-Tirmidhi*.

34. Abu Ishaq, Ibrahim bin Muhammad Al-Isfara'ini. Died 417AH/1026CE. He was born in Isfara'in, between Nishapur and Jurjan. He taught and wrote in Nishapur and his works include a book on the Principles of *fiqh*, and another on theology, *Al-Jaami' fi Usool-ud-Deen*, in five volumes.

35. Ash-Shawkani, Imam Ali bin Muhammad bin Abdullah, from Yemen. Lived 1173-1250AH (1777-1834CE), a great Mujtahid scholar who studied under a number of great scholars. The author of *Nayl Al-Autar* amongst many other books covering all Islamic sciences.

36. Muhammad bin Al-Hasan Ash-Shaibani. Born in the city of Wasith in 132AH/749CE, he settled with his family in Kufa, Iraq. Throughout his life, he had the honour of studying under Imam Abu Haneefah, Imam Malik and Imam Abdullah bin Al-Mubarak. He was a close friend of Imam Ash-Shafi. He was regarded as a 'writing machine' and would sleep very little at night. He is said to have over 1000 compilations attributed to him. He is known as the most authentic collector of the Hanafi school of thought. He died in 189AH/806CE, at the age of 57.

37. Ibn Al-Qasim Al-Maliki, one of the two famous students of Imam Malik, who was responsible for documenting his school of thought and Al-Muwatta. Ibn Abdul-Barr said of him, *"He was a faqih dominated by opinion. He was a righteous, poor, steadfast man."* He was a generous and abstemious man. He did not accept the stipends of any ruler, but would keep away from them. He is reported to have said, *"There is no good in being close to the rulers."* He died in 191AH/806CE at the age of 63.

38. Ibn Al-Qayyim, Abu Abdullah Al-Jawziyyah, was born in Damascus in 691AH/1292CE. He was a Hanbali scholar who authored many famous books, such as the famous *Zad Al-Ma'ad* and *Madarij As-Salikeen*. Being one of Ibn Taymiyyah's best students, he edited his teacher's works and went to prison with him in Damascus,

remaining with him until Ibn Taymiyyah's death in 728AH/1328CE. Ibn Al-Qayyim died in Damascus in 751AH/1350CE.

39. Ibn Hajar Al-Haithami, Ahmad bin Muhammad. Born in 909AH/1504CE in Abu Haytam, Western Egypt, he was the Shafi Imam of his time. He received permission to give *fatawa* when he was barely 20. He died in Makkah in 974AH/1567CE. He wrote many definitive works on Shafi *fiqh*, especially *Minhaj At-Talibeen*, *Tuhfah Al-Muhtaj*, *Al-Fatawa Al-Kubara* and *Az-Zawajir*.

40. Mujahid bin Jubair Al-Makki. Lived 21-104AH/642-722CE and was the most eminent student of the great commentator of the Quran, Abdullah bin Abbas. His wrote a commentary on the Quran: *Tafseer Mujahid*.

41. Abu Dawud, Sulaiman bin Al-Ash'ath bin Ishaq Al-Azdi As-Sijistani, who was one of the eminent Imams of *hadith*, was born in 202H/817CE. He studied *hadith* under Imam Ahmad bin Hanbal along with Al-Bukhari and taught many of the later scholars of *hadith*, like At-Tirmidhi and An-Nasa'i. Though Abu Dawud collected 500,000 *hadith*, he only included 4800 *hadith* in his book entitled *As-Sunan*. He died in Basra on Friday, in the month of Shawwal 275AH/890CE.

42. At-Tirmidhi, Abu Isa Muhammad bin Isa bin Thawra, was born in 209AH/824CE in a town called Tirmiz in Uzbekistan near the northern border of Afghanistan. He was a student of Al-Bukhari, and compiled 4000 *hadith* in his book called Al-Jami which later came to be known As-Sunan At-Tirmidhi. He was famous for his piety. He became blind and finally died on 13 Rajab 279H/894CE.

43. An-Nasa'i, Abu Abdur-Rahman Ahmad bin Ali bin Shuaib bin Ali Al-Hafiz, was born in 215AH/830CE in Nasa', a city in Khurasan. He was one of the Imams of *hadith* and he compiled his book, *Sunan An-Nasa'i*, which is considered third to Saheeh Al-Bukhari in terms of containing the least weak *hadith*. He lived in Egypt then moved to Damascus in Syria and died in Makkah in the year 303AH/918CE.

44. Ibn Majah, Abu Abdullah Muhammad bin Yazid bin Majah Al-Qizwini was born in 207AH/822CE. He studied under Imam Malik and others, and many people narrated *hadith* from him. He was one of the eminent scholars of *hadith*. Ibn Majah died in Ramadan in 273AH/888CE.

45. Al-Baihaqi, Abu Bakr Ahmad bin Al-Hussain, was born in Sha'ban in the year 374AH/987CE. He was considered a learned memoriser among the eminent Imams of *hadith* and a jurisprudence scholar in the

Shafi school of thought. He wrote many books like *As-Sunan Al-Kubara* and *As-Sunan As-Sughra*. Adh-Dhahabi said about him, *"His books exceed one thousand volumes."* Al-Baihaqi, which he is named after, is a town near Nishapur in modern day Iran. Al-Baihaqi died in 458AH/1071CE.

46. Al-Haakim, Abu Abdullah Muhammad Abdullah An-Nishapuri, also known as Ibn Al-Baiyi', was born in 321AH/934CE. He was a celebrated Imam in the verification of *hadith*. He authored *Al-Mustadrak* in the methodology of *hadith*. It is said that he studied under one thousand professors and authored many valuable books. Al-Haakim was known for his piety. He died in Safar 405AH/1018CE.

47. Ad-Darimi, Abu Muhammad Abdullah bin Abdur-Rahman bin Al-Fadl bin Bahram At-Tamimi Ad-Darimi As-Samarqandi, was born in the year 181AH/796CE. He was a celebrated Imam, memoriser and Sheikh-ul-Islam of Samarqand and the author of *Al-Musnad Al-Aali*. Muslim, Abu Dawud, At-Tirmidhi, An-Nasa'i and others transmitted *hadith* from him. He was described to be very intelligent and very virtuous and was considered to be an exemplary person in piousness, patience, hardwork, worship and abstinence. Ad-Darimi died on 8th Dhul-Hijjah 255AH/870CE.

48. At-Tabarani, Abul-Qasim Sulaiman bin Ahmad bin Ayub bin Mutair Al-Lakhmi At-Tabarani, was born in 260AH/875CE in Tabariyyah in Palestine. He was an authoritative Imam and narrated hadith from more than one thousand scholars. He left Ash-Sham to acquire the knowledge of hadith and spent 33 years of travelling in its pursuance. He authored many interesting books, among them are Al-Mu'jam Al-Kabir, Al-Mu'jam Al-Awsat, and Al-Mu'jam As-Sagheer. At-Tabarani lived in Isfahan, Iran, and died there on 27th Dhul-Qa'dah, 360AH/975CE.

49. Ibn Adee, Abu Ahmad Abdullah bin Adee Al-Jurjani, was born in 279AH/894CE. He was a famous Imam, an eminent memoriser and one of the celebrated scholars. Ibn Adee died in 365AH/980CE.

50. Ibn Asakir Ad-Dimashqi, Abul-Qasim Ali bin Al-Hasan bin Hibatullah bin Abdullah Thiqatudeen. Lived 499-571AH/1105-1176CE, he was the Imam of hadith masters in his time and the historian of Damascus. Born in a family of knowledge, he began his studies at the age of six. By the time he reached puberty, he had already attained hadith certifications from the scholars of Damascus, Baghdad and Khurasan. He shunned all kinds of material possessions and

turned down the office of Head Preacher, concentrating on teaching, writing and worshipping. He authored over a hundred books, including the notorious Tareekh Dimashq, a collection of over 80 volumes. His most famous student was the commander, Salahudeen Ayyubi, Conqueror of Jerusalem, who attended Ibn Asakir's funeral when he died. He was buried in Damascus.

51. Adh-Dhahabi, Shamsudeen Muhammad bin Ahmad bin Uthman bin Qaymaz. Born in 673AH/1274CE in Damascus, he was a perspicuous critic and expert examiner of hadith, encyclopedic historian and biographer, and foremost authority in Ilm Ar-Rijaal, the part of hadith Science that deals with the judgement of the narrators of the sayings of the Prophet. He sought knowledge from more than 30 different towns. Ibn Hajar Al-Asqalani is reported to have said upon drinking water from the well of Zamzam in Makkah, "I asked Allah to grant me the ability to reach Adh-Dhahabi's rank in the Science of the hadith." Adh-Dhahabi wrote dozens of books, amongst them the famous Siyar A'laam An-Nubala (Lives of the Elite of the Nobility) and Tareekh Al-Islam (History of Islam), which, with more than 30 volumes each, are monumental encyclopedias of biographical history. He lost his sight just before he died in Damascus, in 748AH/1349CE.

APPENDIX C: The Islamic Ruling on Martyrdom Operations

This article originally appeared in Arabic on the Sawt-ul-Qoqaz (Voice of the Caucasus) web-site, Qoqaz.com, in the year 2000, after a series of martyrdom operations carried out by a young Chechen Muslim woman, Hawwa Barayev, and other Chechen Mujahideen. It was written and checked by a council of learned scholars in the Arabian Peninsula and deals with the subject of martyrdom operations in general, whether they are permissible or not.

Introduction

All Praise is due to Allah, Sustainer of the Universe, Who informs us that:

"Were it not for Allah's repelling some people by means of others, the earth would surely have become corrupt." **[Quran 2:251]**

The choicest peace and blessings be on the Chief of the Prophets, who has said:

"By [Allah] in Whose Hand is my soul! I wish to be killed in the Path of Allah, then brought to life, then killed [again], then brought to life, then killed!" [Bukhari, Muslim and others]

And who has also said, *"Act, and each will be eased to that for which he was created."* [Bukhari, Muslim and others]

Allah legislated Jihad for the dignity of this Ummah, knowing that it is abhorrent to us. People today have neglected this great duty, and pursued what they love, thinking good lies in what they love, and failing to realise that good lies in that which Allah has legislated.

Allah has blessed us, here in Chechnya, by allowing us to fight unbelief - represented by the Russian Army, and we ask Allah to strengthen and assist us. We praise Allah also for allowing us to have scored victories over the enemy. Some of us have fulfilled their pledges; others are still waiting. Verily, Allah has fulfilled His Promise to us, and granted us dignity through Jihad. Our martyred brothers have written, with their blood, a history we can be proud of, and their sacrifices only increase us in eagerness for our own martyrdom, so as to meet Allah, and to be resurrected with the Prophet (SAWS), his Companions and all the other prophets, martyrs and righteous ones.

The Ummah has become used to hearing, throughout its history, about men who sacrifice their lives for the religion, but they are not as familiar with women doing the same. The young woman who was martyred, Hawwa Barayev, is one of the few women whose name will be recorded in history. Undoubtedly, she has set the most marvellous example by her sacrifice. The Russians may well await death from every quarter now, and their hearts may appropriately be filled with terror on account of women like her. Let every jealous one perish in his rage! Let every sluggish individual bury his head in the dirt! She has done what few men have done. Every supporter of the truth should prepare to give the like of what she has given. The Ummah may well be proud that such a paragon has appeared in our midst. We are certain that an Ummah that contains people like her will never - by Allah's leave - become devoid of good.

However, while we were in the midst of rejoicing over our sister's self-sacrifice, and we were still supplicating for her to achieve forgiveness and mercy from Allah, we received mail that clouded our joy. It came, not from an enemy or envier, but rather from a handful of people whom we presume wanted to offer constructive advice. However, they erred, and accused the great Mujahidah, Hawwa Barayev, of having committed suicide, saying that it was not permissible for her to have acted thus. Nor did they think it was permissible for us to mention her account on our website, rather that we should have criticised her. They mentioned evidences which they had misunderstood to imply what they claimed. In this study, we shall clarify that Hawwa Barayev - and similarly Abdur-Rahman Shishani, Qadi Mowladi, Khatam, his brother Ali, Abdul-Malik and others - are, Allah willing, in Gardens of Eternity, in the bodies of green birds, betaking themselves to lanterns hanging from the Throne of Allah. This is how we regard them, but we do not sanctify anyone before Allah.

Before we embark on a detailed exposition concerning the Islamic verdict on martyrdom operations, it is appropriate for us to first present a brief, to-the-point response:

Firstly: If you did not know, could you not ask? It is not appropriate for someone who is unaware of a verdict to make sweeping statements accusing others of wrongdoing. If those who criticised us had only investigated the issue first, they would have found that the issue is, at worst, a disagreed issue among scholars, such that we cannot be criticised for following legitimate scholarship.

Secondly: We request our respected brothers, who seek the truth, not to criticise us for anything without backing the criticism with verdicts of scholars, and [especially] the understanding of the Pious Predecessors.

Thirdly: Dear brothers and sisters! Not every martyrdom operation is legitimate, nor is every martyrdom operation prohibited. Rather, the verdict differs based on factors such as the enemy's condition, the situation of the war, the potential martyr's personal circumstances, and the elements of the operation itself. Thus, one may not give a verdict on such operations without having an understanding of the actual situation, and this is obtained from the Mujahideen, and not the unbelievers. How, then, can you accuse us of ignorance when you are unaware of our situation, let alone the specific details of the operation in question?

Definition of Martyrdom Operations and their Effect on the Enemy

Martyrdom or self-sacrifice operations are those performed by one or more people, against enemies far outstripping them in numbers and equipment, with prior knowledge that the operations will almost inevitably lead to death.

The form this usually takes nowadays is to wire up one's body, or a vehicle or suitcase with explosives, and then to enter amongst a conglomeration of the enemy, or in their vital facilities, and to detonate in an appropriate place there in order to cause the maximum losses in the enemy ranks, taking advantage of the element of surprise and penetration. Naturally, the enactor of the operation will usually be the first to die.

Another technique is for an armed Mujahid to break into the enemy barracks, or area of conglomeration, and fire at them at close-range, without having prepared any plan of escape, nor having considered escape a possibility. The objective is to kill as many of the enemy as possible, and he will almost certainly die.

The name 'suicide-operations' used by some is inaccurate, and in fact this name was chosen by the Jews to discourage people from such endeavours. How great is the difference between one who commits suicide - because of his unhappiness, lack of patience and weakness or absence of Iman and has been threatened with Hell-Fire - and between the self-sacrificer who embarks on the operation out of strength of faith and conviction, and to bring victory to Islam, by sacrificing his life for the upliftment of Allah's Word!

As for the effects of these operations on the enemy, we have found, through the course of our experience that there is no other technique which strikes as much terror into their hearts, and which shatters their spirit as much. On account of this they refrain from mixing with the population, and from oppressing, harassing and looting them. They have also become occupied with trying to expose such operations before they occur, which has distracted them from other things. Praise is to Allah. Many of their imminent plans were foiled, and furthermore, President Putin issued a severe condemnation of the Home Affairs and Defence Ministers, placing the responsibility on them, and threatening high-level reshufflings in the two ministries. Those troops who are not busy trying to foil martyrdom operations are occupied with removal of Russian corpses, healing the wounded, and drawing out plans and policies from beneath the debris. This is all on the moral level.

On the material level, these operations inflict the heaviest losses on the enemy, and are lowest in cost to us. The cost of equipment is negligible in comparison to the assault; in fact the explosives and vehicles were captured as war-booty, such that we returned them to the Russians in our special way! The human casualty is a single life, who is in fact a martyr and hero gone ahead to Gardens of Eternity, insha-Allah. As for the enemy, their losses are high; after the last operation, they had over 1,600 dead and wounded, and the most crucial concentration of Russian forces in Chechnya was completely destroyed.

All of this was achieved by the efforts of only four heroes. We feel sure that the Russians will not remain long in our land with such operations continuing. Either they will fear aggregation, in which case they will become easy targets for attack, or they will gather together to combat the assaults, in which case the martyrdom operations will be sufficient - Allah willing - to disperse them. If they wish to keep matters under control, they would need more than 300,000 troops in every city, and this is no exaggeration.

One can see how much fear the operations in Palestine caused, and that they were a major factor in convincing the Jews to grant self-rule to the Palestinians, hoping that they could be more easily controlled in that way. In Chechnya, the damage is much greater than in similar operations in Palestine, on account of Russian fortification being much less than that possessed by the Jews.

Evidences for the Issue

Before going into the verdict concerning the operations, citing the pronouncements of scholars about them, and resolving some unclear issues, it is appropriate for us to first present some of the Shariah (Islamic law) evidences, and then follow them up with discussion and application thereof. We will not analyse the chains of transmission of each narration separately; we will regard it as sufficient that the basis of the evidence is in the collections of Bukhari and Muslim, and hence any reports outside of these two books is strengthened by them.

1. "*Verily, Allah has purchased from the believers their selves and their wealth, in return for Paradise being theirs. They fight in the path of Allah and they kill and are killed.*" [Quran 9:111]

Hence, any scenario in which the Mujahid offers the purchase price in order to attain the merchandise is permissible unless an evidence exists to specifically prohibit it.

2. *"How many a small force has overcome a numerous force, by the Permission of Allah. And Allah is with the steadfast ones."* [Quran 2:249]

This verse indicates that the measure of power in the Shariah is not primarily linked to material, worldly measures.

3. *"Among mankind is he who sells himself seeking the pleasure of Allah. And Allah is Merciful towards His servants."* [Quran 2:207]

According to the explanation of this verse by the Sahabah, as we cite below, one who sells himself for the sake of Allah is not considered to have committed suicide, even if he immerses himself into 1,000 of the enemy forces without armour.

4. In the hadith in Saheeh Muslim, containing the account of the Boy and the King in the story of the Trenches referred to by Surah Al-Buruj, we find that the unbelieving King tried various means to kill the believing Boy, failing each time. Eventually, the Boy told him, *"You will not be able to kill me until you gather people on one plateau, hang me on a palm-trunk, take an arrow from my quiver, place it in the bow, say, 'In the name of Allah, the Lord of the boy' and shoot me."* The King did this, and thereby managed to kill the Boy as predicted, but the people who had gathered began saying, *"We believe in Allah, the Lord of the Boy!"* Thereupon, the King ordered trenches to be dug, and fires lit in them, and then for the people to be made to jump into them if they refused to give up their faith. This was done, and eventually a woman was brought with her infant, and she hesitated to jump on account of him, but he said, *"O mother! Remain steadfast for you are upon the truth."*

The Boy, in this hadith, ordered the King to kill him in the interest of the religion, and this indicates that such a deed is legitimate, and not considered suicide.

5. Imam Ahmad has narrated in his *Musnad* (1/310) [and a similar narration is in *Ibn Majah* (4030)] that Ibn Abbas said that the Messenger of Allah (SAWS) said, "On the night in which I was taken by night, a pleasant fragrance came my way, and so I said, *'O Gabriel! What is this pleasant fragrance?'* He said, *'This is the fragrance of the hairdresser of Pharaoh's daughter, and [of the hairdresser]'s children.'* I said, *'What is her situation?'* He said, *'While she was combing Pharaoh's daughter's hair one day, the comb fell from her hand, so she said, 'In the name of Allah'*" Pharaoh's daughter asked, *'[You mean] my father?'* She said, *'No, rather my Lord, and the Lord of your father, is Allah.'* She said, *'Can I tell him that?'* She said, *'Yes.'"* The hadith goes on to describe that a huge brass pot was heated, and it was ordered for her and her children to be cast therein. She requested from Pharaoh - and he acceded to her request - that her bones and her children's bones be gathered in a single cloth and buried. Her children were then thrown into the cauldron one by one before her eyes, until they got to a suckling infant, and it seemed she wavered on account of him, but he said, *'O mother! Jump in, for the torture of this world is lighter than the punishment of the Hereafter.'* So she jumped in."

The narrators of the chain [of Imam Ahmad's version] are reliable, apart from Abu Umar Ad-Dareer, whom Adh-Dhahabi and Abu Hatim Ar-Razi considered truthful, and Ibn Hibban considered reliable.

According to this hadith, the child was made to speak, as was the child in the preceding story of the trenches, telling the mother to jump into the fire, which indicates the virtue of this deed.

6. Abu Dawud (3/27) and At-Tirmidhi (4/280) have narrated (and At-Tirmidhi graded it as Saheeh) that Aslam bin Imran narrated that when they were fighting a mighty army of the Romans, a man in the Muslim army attacked the Roman ranks until he penetrated them. People shouted, saying, *"Subhan-Allah! He has contributed to his own destruction."* Thereupon, Abu Ayub Al-Ansari stood up, and said, *"O people! You give this interpretation to this verse, whereas it was revealed concerning us, the Ansar. When Allah had given honour to Islam and its supporters had become many, some of us secretly said to one another ... 'Our wealth has been depleted, and Allah has given honour to Islam and its supporters have become many, so let us stay amidst our wealth and make up what has been depleted of it.' Thereupon, Allah revealed to His Prophet [meaning]* "**And spend in the Path of Allah, and do not contribute to your own destruction...**" [Quran 2:195] *refuting what we*

had said. So, the destruction lay in staying with our wealth and hoarding it, and abandoning combat." Abu Ayub remained fixed until he [was killed and] was buried in Rome.

Al-Haakim authenticated it, saying it conforms to the criteria of Bukhari and Muslim, and Adh-Dhahabi corroborated him. An-Nasa'i and Ibn Hibban also narrated it. Al-Baihaqi included it, and other narrations in his Sunan in a chapter entitled, *"Permissibility of a man or men fighting alone in the enemy land"* thereby citing it as evidence for the permissibility of advancing against a group, even if the more likely result is that they will kill him.

In this hadith, Abu Ayub explained that the verse **[Quran 2:195]** does not apply to one who plunges into the enemy ranks alone, even though it may seem to people that he is destroying himself. The Sahabah tacitly confirmed this explanation of his [by not objecting].

7. Ibn Abi Shaibah has narrated in his *Musannaf* (5/338) that Muadh bin Afra asked the Messenger of Allah, *"What makes Allah laugh upon His slave?"* The reply: *"[The servant] immersing himself into the enemy without armour."* Muadh then took off his armour and fought until he was killed.

This hadith is a clear evidence for the virtue of Jihad operations in which it is most likely that one will die, and it indicates that Jihad has some special rules which permit what may normally be prohibited.

8. Ibn Abi Shaibah has extracted (5/289) [and similarly At-Tirmidhi (2491 and 2492, the latter narration he classified as Saheeh) and An-Nasa'i (1597 and 2523), and Ahmad (20/393), as well as At-Tabarani (in *Al-Kabir*, with a hasan chain) and Abdullah bin Al-Mubarak (in *Kitab Al-Jihad*, 1/84)], *"Three [categories of people] Allah loves,..."* and among them is *"a man who was in a dispatchment and met the enemy, and they were defeated, but he faced them with his chest until he was killed or victorious."* Al-Haakim also narrated it, and said it is Saheeh.

9. Ahmad narrated in his Musnad (6/22) from Ibn Masood that the Prophet (SAWS) said, *"Our Sustainer marvels at two men: a man who stirs from his bed ... to salah ... and a man who fights in the path of Allah, and his*

companions are defeated, and he realises what awaits him in defeat and what awaits him in returning [to combat], but he returns [to combat] until his blood is spilled. Allah says, **'Look at My servant who went back [to combat] hopeful and anxious for what is with Me, until his blood was spilled.'"**

Ahmad Shakir said its chain is Saheeh. Haithami said in *Majma Az-Zawa'id*: Ahmad and Abu Ya'la narrated it, as did At-Tabarani in *Al-Kabir*, and its isnad is hasan. Abu Dawud and Al-Haakim narrated it in abbreviated form, and Al-Haakim authenticated it. Ibn Nuhaas said: *"Even if there were only this single authentic hadith, it would suffice us as evidence for the virtue of plunging [into the enemy ranks]."*

10. Muslim has narrated from Abu Hurairah, *"Among the best of lives for people is a man who clasps the reins of his horse in the path of Allah, rushing on its back; whenever he hears a cry [of battle] or advancement towards the enemy, he hurries to it, seeking death and being slain with eagerness."*

This indicates that seeking to be killed and pursuing martyrdom are legitimate and praiseworthy acts.

11. Al-Baihaqi has narrated in *Al-Sunan Al-Kubara* (9/100) with a Saheeh chain from Mujahid that the Prophet sent out Abdullah bin Masood and Khabbab as one dispatchment, and Dihyah as a dispatchment on his own.

This indicates that regardless of the level of risk in a Jihad operation, it remains permissible by default, and the greater the risk, the greater the reward.

12. Bukhari and Muslim have narrated that Talhah shielded the Prophet from arrows in the Battle of Uhud, and his hand was crippled thereby.

13. Bukhari and Muslim have reported that Salamah bin Al-Akwa' was asked, *"For what did you pledge allegiance to the Prophet on the Day of Hudaybiyyah?"* He said, *"For death."*

70

14. Many have reported from Muhammad bin Thabit bin Qays bin Shimas, when the Muslims were beaten back on the Day of the Battle of Yamamah, Salim, the freed-slave of Abu Hudhaifah, said, *"This is not how we used to act with the Messenger of Allah."* Then, he dug a trench for himself, and stood in it carrying the flag, and fought until he was killed as a martyr on the Day of Yamamah.

This and the next report indicate that steadfastness is desirable, even if it leads to death, and Salim attributed this type of action to the [days of] the Messenger of Allah (SAWS).

15. Ibn Jareer At-Tabari has narrated in his *Tareekh* (2/151) that in the Battle of Mu'tah, Jafar bin Abi Talib took the flag and fought until he became immersed in the fighting, whereupon he turned to a light-coloured horse he had and wounded it [so he could not escape], then he fought until he was killed. Hence, Jafar was the first Muslim to wound his horse [in this manner].

16. Muslim has narrated that a man heard a Companion saying, when the enemy was near, *"The Messenger of Allah (SAWS) said : 'The doors of Paradise are under the shades of swords.'"* The man, upon hearing this, got up and asked for verification of the hadith. When it was confirmed, he turned to his companions, gave them the greeting of salam, broke and discarded the scabbard of his sword and then advanced to the enemy with his sword, striking them until he was killed.

[Translator's Note: The original study in Arabic contains 40 narrations, but for brevity we have omitted the remainder].

Verdicts of Scholars Concerning one who Attacks the Enemy Alone

Having established the permissibility of plunging into the enemy and attacking alone even when death is certain, we proceed and say that the martyrdom operations are derived from this principle, realising that the prohibition of suicide relates to deficiency or absence of faith. However, the former generations did not have knowledge of martyrdom operations in their current-day form, for these evolved

71

with the changes in techniques of warfare, and hence they did not specifically address them. However, they did address similar issues, such as that of attacking the enemy single-handed and frightening them with one's own death being certain. They also deduced general principles under which the martyrdom operations fall, and in doing so they relied on evidences such as those we have mentioned in the previous section. There is one difference between the martyrdom operations and their classical precedent, namely that in our case the person is killed by his own hand, whereas in the other he was killed by the enemy. We also explain that this difference does not affect the verdict.

A. Scholars of the Sahabah and Tabi'een

1. Ibn Al-Mubarak and Ibn Abi Shaibah (5/303) have reported, through a Saheeh chain, that Mudrik bin Awf Al-Ahmasi said, *'I was in the presence of Umar when the messenger of Nu'man bin Al-Muqarrin came to him and Umar asked him about the people, whereupon he replied, 'So-and-so and so-and-so were hit, and others and others whom I do not know.' Umar said, 'But Allah knows them.' [The messenger] said, 'O Chief of the believers! [There was] a man who sold his life.' At this, Mudrik said, 'That is my maternal uncle, by Allah, O Chief of the believers! People claimed he has contributed to his own destruction.' Umar said, 'They have lied (or: are mistaken). Rather, he is among those who have bought the Hereafter with this world.'* Al-Baihaqi mentioned that that was on the Day of the Battle of Nihawand.

2. Ibn Abi Shaibah has extracted (5/322) that a battalion of unbelievers advanced, and a man of the Ansar faced them and attacked them, and broke through the ranks, then returned, repeating this twice or thrice. Sad bin Hisham mentioned this to Abu Hurairah, who recited the verse (meaning), **"Among mankind is he who sells himself seeking the pleasure of Allah."**

3. Al-Haakim has extracted in the *Book of Tafseer* (2/275) and Ibn Abi Hatim (1/128), with a similar narration recorded by Ibn Asakir, that Baraa' was asked about the verse (meaning), **"And spend in the Path of Allah, and do not contribute to your own destruction..."**, does it refer to a man who encounters the enemy and fights until he is killed? He said, *"No, rather it is a man who commits a sin, and then says Allah will not*

forgive him." Al-Haakim said this is authentic according to Bukhari's and Muslim's criteria. This explanation of the verse was narrated by At-Tabari in his exegesis (3/584) from Hudhaifah, Ibn Abbas, Ikrimah, Hasan Al-Basri, Ataa', Saeed bin Jubair, Dahhaak, As-Sudi, Muqatil and others.

B. Verdicts of Renowned Exegetes

1. Ibn Al-Arabi says in *Ahkam Al-Quran* (1/116, and see also Al-Qurtubi's *Tafseer* 2/364), commenting on the verse, (meaning), **"And spend in the Path of Allah, and do not contribute to your own destruction..."** *"There are five views about [the meaning of] destruction [here]:*

Do not give up spending [in the path of Allah],
Do not go out without provision,
Do not abandon Jihad,
Do not take on an enemy you are not capable of withstanding,
Do not despair of forgiveness."

At-Tabari said: 'It is general [in scope], and there is no contradiction between them.' He is right, except regarding plunging into the enemy, for scholars have disagreed concerning this. Qasim bin Mukhaimirah, Qasim bin Muhammad and Abdul-Malik from among our [Maliki] scholars said there is no objection to a man single-handedly taking on a large army, if he is strong and [the action] is sincerely for Allah. If he has no power, then that is self-destruction. It has been said [by some] that if he is seeking martyrdom and his intention is sincere, he can attack, for his goal is to kill one of the enemy forces, and that is clear in the verse (meaning), **"Among mankind is he who sells himself seeking the pleasure of Allah."** *The correct view by me is that of permissibility of rushing into an army one cannot withstand, for it contains four [possible] aspects:*

Seeking martyrdom,
Inflicting losses [on the enemy],
Encouraging the Muslims to attack

Demoralizing the enemy, showing them that if one man can do this, what will the totality be capable of!"

2. Al-Qurtubi says in his Tafseer (2/364), "Muhammad bin Al-Hasan Al-Shaibani, the student of Abu Haneefah, said: 'If a man single-handedly attacks 1,000 pagans, there is no objection to it if there is hope of success, or inflicting loss on the enemy, otherwise it is disliked, for then he would expose himself to death without benefit to the Muslims. As for someone whose aim is to embolden the Muslims to emulate his feat, its permissibility is not far-fetched, for it entails benefit to the Muslims in some ways. If his intent is to frighten the enemy, and demonstrate the Muslims' strength of faith, its permissibility is not far-fetched. If there is benefit in it for the Muslims, then giving one's life for the strengthening of the religion and weakening of the unbelievers is the noble rank praised in the verse, (meaning), "Among mankind is he who sells himself seeking the pleasure of Allah." and other verses.'"

3. Ash-Shawkani says in Fath Al-Qadir (1/297) about the verse of self-destruction, "The reality is that the words have general implication and are not specific to the circumstances of revelation. Therefore, everything which may be described as worldly or religious self-destruction is covered by it, as stated by Ibn Jareer At-Tabari. Among that which comes under this verse is a man attacking an enemy army which he can neither overcome, nor have any effect beneficial to the Mujahideen." This implies that if there is a benefit, it is permissible.

C. Texts of the Madhahib

Hanafi

Ibn Abidin says in his Hashiyah (4/303), "There is no objection to a man fighting alone, even if he thinks he will be killed, provided he achieves something such as killing, wounding or defeating [the enemy], for this has been reported from a number of the Sahabah in the presence of the Messenger of Allah on the Day of Uhud, and he praised them for it. If, however, he knows he will not inflict any loss on them, it is not permissible for him to attack, for it would not contribute to the strengthening of the religion."

Maliki

Ibn Khuwayz-Mandad said, as cited by Al-Qurtubi in his *Tafseer* (2/364), *"As for a man single-handedly attacking 100 or more enemy troops ... this has two scenarios: If he is certain, or reasonably so, that he will kill the subject of his attack, and emerge safe, then it is good, and similarly if he is reasonably certain that he will be killed, but will inflict loss or cause damage, or have a beneficial effect for the Muslims, then it is permissible also."* Statements from Al-Qurtubi and Ibn Al-Arabi have already preceded.

Shafi

In the completion of Al-Majmu (19/291) by Al-Muti', we find, *"If the number of the unbelievers are twice the numbers of the Muslims and they do not fear perdition, it is obligatory to stand firm ... If they are more convinced than not of destruction, then there are two possibilities:*

1. *That they may turn back, based on the verse (meaning),* **"do not contribute to your own destruction..."**

2. *That they may not turn back, and this is the correct view, based on the verse, (meaning),* **"When you encounter a force, remain steadfast..."**, *and because the Mujahid only fights in order to kill or be killed. If the number of the unbelievers exceed twice the numbers of the Muslims, then they may turn back. If they are more convinced than not that they will not be destroyed, then it is better for them to remain steadfast so that the Muslims are not routed. If they are more convinced than not that they will be destroyed, then there are two possibilities:*

That they are obliged to turn back, based on the words of Allah (meaning), **"do not contribute to your own destruction..."**

That it is recommended for them to turn back, but not binding, for if they are killed they will attain martyrdom."

Hanbali

Ibn Qudamah says in Al-Mughni (9/309), *"If the enemy is more than twice the Muslims' number, and the Muslims are reasonably certain of victory, then it is preferable to remain steadfast on account of the benefit [involved], but if they turn back it is permissible, for they are not immune to destruction ... it is conceivable that they are obliged to stand fast if they are reasonably certain of victory, on account of the benefit, but if they are reasonably certain of being defeated by remaining and being unscathed by turning back, then it is preferable for them to turn back, but if they remain put, it is permissible, for they have a goal of martyrdom, and it is also possible that they will be victorious. If they are reasonably certain of being routed whether they remain put or turn back, then it is preferable for them to remain steadfast to attain the rank of martyrdom, ... and also because it is possible they might be victorious."*

Ibn Taymiyyah says, in *Majmu' Al-Fatawa* (28/540), *"Muslim has narrated in his Saheeh, the story of the people of the trenches, in which the Boy ordered his own killing for the benefit of the religion, and hence the four imams have allowed a Muslim to immerse himself in the enemy ranks, even if he is reasonably certain that they will kill him, provided there is benefit in that for the Muslims."*

Zahiri

Ibn Hazm says in Al-Muhalla (7/294), *"Neither Abu Ayub al-Ansari nor Abu Musa Al-Ashari criticised a man plunging alone into a raging army and remaining steadfast until he was killed... It has been authentically reported that a man from among the Sahabah asked the Messenger of Allah (SAWS) about what makes Allah laugh upon a servant and he said, 'His immersing himself into the enemy without armour,' whereupon the man removed his armour and entered the enemy [ranks, fighting] until he was killed."*

D. Some Analysis

The hadith of the Boy is the strongest of evidences for this issue. The hadith explains that when the Boy saw that his being killed in a specific way would be a means for spreading the religion, and hence he advised the King - from whom Allah had protected him hitherto - how to kill him, for the spreading of the religion and peoples entering into it was more weighty in his eyes than his remaining alive, and he thereby contributed to taking his own life. Yes, he did not take it by his own hand, but his opinion was the sole factor leading to his killing. This is just as if a man, suffering from painful wounds, asked someone else to kill him; he would be as guilty of suicide as if he had taken his own life, regardless of who did the killing, for he requested it. Similarly, Allah praised those who believed in the Boy's Lord; those who were being forced to jump into the pits of fire for refusing to renounce their faith. Nay, even the infant spoke, encouraging its mother to advance when she hesitated about entering the fire. They were praised in Surah Al-Buruj, which described their fate as being gardens beneath which flow rivers, and they are called successful. The story of Pharaoh's daughter's hairdresser is similar. We have cited evidences from our Shariah which fortify these two hadiths, and nothing has appeared to contradict sacrificing one's life for raising Allah's Word. Hence, the content of these two hadiths is part of our Shariah, according to the majority of scholars.

In fact, we see that this sort of operation was carried out in the presence of the Prophet (SAWS), and after him by the Sahabah, not once but many times. Furthermore, protection of the religion is the greatest service a Mujahid performs and the evidences do not leave us with any doubt that a Mujahid may sacrifice his life for the religion. Talhah shielded the Prophet (SAWS) with his hand, and this supports the permissibility of a person sacrificing himself for others in the interests of the religion.

E. Synopsis

It has transpired that scholars gave, to the issue of plunging single-handed into the enemy with reasonable certainty of being killed, the same verdict as in cases of death being certain, such that whoever permits the latter permits the former. Further, the majority of scholars gave conditions for the permissibility:

Intention,
Infliction of losses on the enemy,
Frightening them,
Strengthening the hearts of the Muslims.

Al-Qurtubi and Ibn Qudamah allowed plunging into the enemy with only a sincere intention, even if no other conditions are fulfilled, for seeking martyrdom is legitimate. Since there is no explicit stipulation of the majority's conditions in narrations, this view appears preferable. The majority deduced their conditions from general standards of the Shariah, but the general need not restrict the specific. Yes, we do say that if there is no benefit to the Muslims or the Mujahideen, an action should not be carried out, and is not the most optimal practice, but this is apart from the original permissibility of the act, for to condemn one seeking martyrdom without a firm basis is an injustice.

The Issue of using Prisoners as a Human Shield

The issue of killing Muslim prisoners whom the enemy has used as a human shield resembles the issue at hand, although there is also a difference between them. The similarity is that both involve ending a Muslim life in the interests of the religion. The difference between the issues is that killing those used as a shield was permitted by scholars out of necessity, for there does not exist any text permitting the taking of someone else's life, rather it derives from the public interest overshadowing the individual interest. Hence, killing prisoners used as a shield is based on the rule of necessity permitting the unlawful, and of choosing the lesser of two evils when one is inevitable. As for martyrdom operations, no such rules need be applied, for we have clear texts encouraging plunging into the enemy ranks in spite of the certainty of being killed, and it is not a case of necessity.

Killing another person is an even greater sin than killing oneself. Al-Qurtubi cites in his *Tafseer* (10/183) the consensus of scholars that anyone who is coerced to kill someone else may not comply. Hence whoever allows killing another Muslim, where no textual evidence exists, but for an overwhelming religious benefit, should similarly allow killing oneself for an overwhelming benefit, for the taking of one's own life is less serious than taking someone else's life. This would be even if we did not have any texts to support martyrdom operations, although we actually do have specific evidences, as mentioned earlier.

The Muslim army is ordinarily prohibited from killing not only Muslims, but also dhimmis (unbelievers living as protected subjects of the Muslim state), as well as old men, women and children from among the unbelievers. If Muslim prisoners of war are used by the unbelievers then it is not permissible to fire on them except in cases of dire necessity. In the case of women and children of the unbelievers, however, they could be fired upon for an expediency of war even if it is not dire necessity, for war may need such action, but the intention should not be specifically to kill the non-combatants. The Prophet (SAWS) was asked about the pagans being hit by night, and some women and children being killed in the process, and he replied, *"They are from among them."* [Bukhari and Muslim] In the case of Muslims, however, firing is permissible only if abstaining will lead to a wholesale harm, such as a greater number of Muslims being killed than those being used as a shield, or the Muslims being defeated and their land overrun. In such a case, any Muslims killed as a result will be raised up according to their intentions.

The majority consider it obligatory to attack the enemy in cases of necessity, even if it leads to the members of a human shield being killed. [See: Ash-Shawkani's *Fath Al-Qadir* (5/447), *Mughni Al-Muhtaj* (4/244), *Hashiyah Ad-Dussuqi* (2/178), and Ibn Qudamah's *Al-Mughni* (10/505)] The author of *Mughni Al-Muhtaj* gives two conditions which should be satisfied:

1. That the Mujahideen try their best to avoid hitting the shield deliberately.
2. That they do not intend to kill the people in the shield.

Ibn Taymiyyah said, *"If the unbelievers use Muslims as a human shield, and the unbelievers cannot be repelled without killing [the Muslims], then [the Muslim army may fire], for inflictions and afflictions may smite one in this world who does not deserve it in the Hereafter, and it counts as a misfortune for him [for which he may be rewarded]. Some expressed this by saying, 'The killer is a Mujahid and the killed one is a martyr.'"*

The majority of Hanafis and Malikis, as well as Imam Sufyan Ath-Thawri, have permitted attacking when the enemy have used a shield of Muslims, whether or not abstaining would be detrimental or lead to defeat, reasoning that otherwise Jihad would never take place. [See: *Fath Al-Qadir* (5/448), *Al-Jassas's Ahkam Al-Quran* (5/273) and *Minah Al-Jaleel* (3/151)] The weakness of this position is clear, in that the sanctity of a Muslim life is greater than to allow its taking without a clear proof, and moreover such shields are not universally used, and so Jihad would not necessarily come to a halt.

In the case of women, children and old men from among the unbelievers being used as a shield, the majority of Hanafis, Shafi's and Hanbalis have allowed attacking even if it is not a dire necessity. [See: *As-Siyar Al-Kabeer* (4/1554) *Mughni Al-Muhtaj* (4/224) and *Al-Mughni* (10/504)] The Malikis differed, but for brevity we will not mention their reasoning. [See: Dardeer's *Ash-Sharh Al-Kabeer* (2/178) and *Minah Al-Jaleel* (3/150).]

The View of the Majority Concerning one who Assists in Killing

Plunging into the enemy ranks without hope of escape is the greatest means by which a Mujahid contributes to his death, and contributing to one's own death is just like killing oneself, just as one who deliberately causes the death of someone is like one who actually killed him. The majority of scholars, from among the Malikis, Shafi's and Hanbalis, have subjected one who kills someone by consequence to being killed in retaliation just as in the case of direct murder.

Among the textual bases for this is that which Bukhari has reported, that a boy was assassinated, whereupon Umar said, *"Even if all the inhabitants of Sanaa took part in it, I would kill them all."* From a rational angle, if killing in retaliation were to be halted in such a case, murder would increase, for murderers would merely use one or more accomplices, without fear of being executed for the crime. The monetary compensation of blood-money would not deter all murderers, especially the well-off. Hence it is fitting for all the participants to be executed, and in a similar light the Quran describes one who kills one person to be like one who has killed all mankind. [See: *As-Sayl Al-Jarrar* (4/397), *Tafseer Al-Qurtubi* (2/251), *Majmu' Fatawa Ibn Taymiyyah* (20/382), *Al-Bahr Ar-Ra'iq* (8/354), *Sam'ani's Qawati Al-Adillah* (2/243)]

80

Therefore, if one who kills himself by plunging into the enemy is praised, then this praise applies independent of the weapon and manner in which he gives up his life. We have already mentioned in Evidence 14, the Sahabi's action, and no criticism or stipulation has been recorded from the Prophet (SAWS) of such a practice. Hence, if allowing oneself to be killed by the enemy is allowed when it is in the interests of the Muslims, then clearly killing oneself for the same purpose should be allowed, and in such a case a Mujahid is exempted from the general texts which prohibit taking one's own life.

Definition of a Shaheed (martyr)

Imam An-Nawawi has enumerated [in *Sharh Saheeh Muslim* (1/515) and *Al-Majmu* (1/277)] seven explanations for why the martyr is called Shaheed:

Because Allah and the Prophet have testified concerning his entry into Paradise,
Because he is alive before his Lord,
Because the angels of mercy witness the taking of his soul,
Because he will be among those who testify over nations on the Day of Resurrection,
Because his faith and good ending have outwardly been witnessed,
Because he has a witness to his death on Iman, namely his blood,
Because his soul immediately witnesses Paradise.

Ibn Hajar has mentioned fourteen means by which a person can acquire the title, some of them specifically related to being killed in the path of Allah and others not. [See: *Fath Al-Bari* (6/43)]

Jurists have given the technical definition of a martyr as follows:

According to the Hanafis:

"One who is killed by the pagans, or is found killed in the battle bearing a mark of any wound, whether external or internal - such as blood emerging from an eye or the like." [*Al-Inayah* published on the margins of *Fath Al-Qadir* (2/142) and Hashiyah Ibn Abidin (2/268)]

"Anyone who is killed while fighting pagans, or rebels, or brigands, by a means attributed to the enemy - whether directly or by consequence - is a shaheed. Anyone who is killed by a means not specifically attributed to [an action of] the enemy is not considered a shaheed." [Zaylai's *Tabi'een Al-Haqa'iq*, (1/247). See also *Al-Bahr Al-Ra'iq* (2/211)]

According to the Malikis:

"One who is killed while fighting warring unbelievers only, even if killed on Islamic land, such as if the enemy attacked the Muslims, [even if he] did not fight on account of being unaware or asleep, [and even if] killed by a Muslim who mistook him for an unbeliever, or trampled by a horse, or mistakenly smitten by his own sword or arrow, or by having fallen into a well or from a cliff during the fighting." [Dardeer's *Al-Sharh Al-Kabeer* (1/425)]

According to the Shafi's:

"One who is killed in fighting unbelievers, facing and not running away, for the raising of Allah's Word...and not for any worldly motive." [Mughni *Al-Muhtaj* (1/350) and see *Fath Al-Bari* (6/129)]

According to the Hanbalis:

"One who dies in a battle with the unbelievers, whether male or female, adult or not, whether killed by the unbelievers, or by his own weapon in error, or by having fallen off his mount, or having been found dead with no mark, provided he was sincere." [*Kash-shaf Al-Qina'*, 2/113. See also *Al-Mughni* (2/206)]

From the above, it transpires that the majority - apart from the Hanafis - do not consider the identity of the killing party to be a factor in determining whether the victim is a shaheed. The majority view emerges preferable, based on:

i. A hadith narrated by Bukhari (4196) in which Amir, while trying to kill an enemy man during the Battle of Khaibar, mistakenly killed himself instead. Someone said he had invalidated his good deeds, but the Prophet (SAWS) said, *"Whoever says that, is lying (or mistaken). Verily, he is has two rewards,"* and he coupled two of his fingers, *"He was a perservering Mujahid and there are few Arabs who achieved the like of (good deeds) that Amir has done."*

ii. A hadith narrated by Abu Dawud (2539) about a Companion who mistakenly hit himself with his own sword and people asked, *"Is he a shaheed?"*, whereupon it is reported that the Prophet (SAWS) said, *"Yes, and I am a witness for him."*

Some people may waver about the permissibility of martyrdom operations because the Mujahid is killing himself. In order to dispel this confusion, we may remind ourselves that the Shariah often gives a differing verdict about two actions which externally appear the same, but differ in the intentions behind them. For example:

Marrying a divorced woman is permissible, but doing so with the sole intention of making her permissible to the first husband is prohibited.
Paying back a loan with more than was borrowed is allowed, but if the excess is stipulated in the contract, it is prohibited, being riba.
One who performs Jihad in order to raise aloft the Word of Allah is a Mujahid, but one who fights for the sake of showing off bravery is among the first who will be taken to Hell.
Mistakenly striking oneself with one's own weapon makes one shaheed (according to the majority) but deliberately killing oneself to escape the pain of wounds makes one deserving of Hell.

These examples, all based on the hadith, *"Verily, actions are only according to intentions…"*, clearly support the notion that the verdict concerning the shaheed does not differ based on who the killing party is, provided the intention is pure. So, one who has a bad intention and is killed by the enemy is deserving of the Fire, as would be the case if he kills himself out of pain. And, one who has a sincere intention will be in Paradise, whether he is killed by the enemy, or kills himself in error. And, one who helps in killing himself for the good of the religion will be in Paradise, like the Boy, insha-Allah.

Definition of Suicide

Suicide here refers to killing oneself on account of anger, pain or some other worldly motive, and scholars are unanimous that it is prohibited

and moreover a major sin, making the offender deserving of Hell -
either eternally if he legitimises the act, or for a finite duration [if he
did not legitimise it and died as a Muslim]. ***"Do not kill yourselves.
Verily, Allah is Merciful to you. And, whoever does that, out of
aggression and injustice, We shall burn him in a Fire. And that is
easy for Allah."*** [Quran 4:29-30; See *Tafseer Al-Qurtubi* (5/156)]

*"Among those before you, there was a man with a wound, and he was in anguish,
so he took a knife and cut his hands, and the blood did not stop until he died.
Allah said,* **"My servant has hastened the ending of his life, so I
have prohibited Paradise to him."** [Bukhari and Muslim]

*"Whoever strangles himself will be strangling himself in the Fire, and whoever stabs
himself will be stabbing himself in the Fire."* [Bukhari and Muslim]

The authentic ahadith on this subject are many. In fact, we have been
ordered not to even wish for death.

*"Let not any of you wish for death on account of harm which has befallen him. But,
if he must, he should pray, 'O Allah! Keep me alive as long as life is better for me,
and take my life when death is better for me."* [Bukhari and Muslim]

All of these texts prohibiting suicide are related to killing oneself for
worldly motives such as pain or anguish or lack of patience, and not
for raising aloft the Word of Allah. We have already cited the
evidences for permitting a Mujahid to plunge into the enemy ranks
without armour, and these exempt the Mujahid from the generality of
the suicide texts. Can one then say that one who kills himself in order
to lift the Word of Allah - to inflict losses on the enemy, to frighten
them, and with a sincere intention - can we describe him as one
committing suicide? That is a grave slander. We say that the
prohibition of suicide is on account of its resulting from weakness or
lack of faith, whereas the Mujahid in a martyrdom operation is killing
himself on account of the strength of his faith. The Boy in the account
of the Trenches referred to in Surah Al-Buruj effectively killed himself
for such a reason, and his deed was praiseworthy. Similarly, the
Prophet (SAWS) wished for death in the Path of Allah, not once but
thrice [the hadith was cited at the start of the article], and it was
permissible because it was not on account of harm which had befallen

him, but rather it emanated from strong faith. So, when the rationale of the prohibition of suicide becomes clear, one arrives at the conclusion that martyrdom operations are permissible and praiseworthy when undertaken for some religious benefit.

Synopsis

We have arrived at the conclusion that martyrdom operations are permissible, and in fact the Mujahid who is killed in them is better than one who is killed fighting in the ranks, for there are gradations even among martyrs, corresponding to their role, action, effort and risk undertaken. Then, we explained how martyrdom operations are the least costly to the Mujahideen and most detrimental to the enemy. We have heard, as you must have, that most scholars today permit such operations: at least 30 Fatawa have been issued to this effect. We explained how this issue is derived from the issue of plunging single-handedly into the enemy ranks; something which is praiseworthy by the agreement of jurists. We then further stated that we preferred the view that such an action is permissible even if martyrdom is the only goal, although it is certainly not the optimal practice. Martyrdom operations should not be carried out unless certain conditions are met:

One's intention is sincere and pure - to raise the Word of Allah.
One is reasonably sure that the desired effect cannot be achieved by any other means which would guarantee preservation of his life.
One is reasonably sure that loss will be inflicted on the enemy, or they will be frightened, or the Muslims will be emboldened.
One should consult with war strategy experts, and especially with the amber of war, for otherwise he may upset plan and alert the enemy to their presence.

If the first condition is absent, the deed is worthless, but if it is satisfied while some others are lacking, then it is not the best thing, but this does not necessarily mean the Mujahid is not shaheed.

We also explained how causing a death carries the same verdict as actual killing. Hence, one who plunges without armour into the enemy ranks, being certain of death, just like one who engages in a martyrdom operation, is effectively causing his own death, but they are praiseworthy because of the circumstances and intention, and hence are not considered to have committed suicide. We also clarified that [according to the majority] the identity of the killer does not have an effect on whether the Mujahid will be considered shaheed. This dispels the wavering arising from the fact that the Mujahid is taking his own life. Thus, such operations could take on any of the five Shari verdicts depending on intention and circumstances. Finally, we clarified that taking one's own life is not always blameworthy; rather it is contingent on the motives behind it. So, we conclude that one who kills himself because of his strong faith and out of love for Allah and the Prophet (SAWS), and in the interests of the religion, is praiseworthy.

Conclusion

Finally, we should point out that this topic needs a much more expansive study. However, we are thankful to Allah for having allowed us to complete this. If we are correct, it is due to Allah, and if we have erred, then all humans are prone to error. Finally, let the scholars and students of knowledge approach us with their feedback and advice, for we are in need of such help. Let them fear Allah in discharging their responsibility to us.

And peace and blessings be upon the Messenger of Allah, who rightly waged Jihad in the Path of Allah until he left this world, and also upon his Household and Companions and those who follow them in goodness until the Day of Judgment.

And our final words are Praise be to Allah, Lord of the Worlds.

APPENDIX D: GLOSSARY

Ansar: anyone of the Companions of the Prophet (SAWS) from the inhabitants of Madinah, who received and hosted the Muslim immigrants from Makkah and other places.

Ahlul-Harb: literally, 'people of war': all people belonging to the nation of the enemy.

Ahlus-Sunnah wal-Jamah: those who follow the authentic Sunnah of the Prophet (SAW) according to the understanding of the Companions of the Prophet (SAWS).

Alim: scholar or man of knowledge.

Amir: chief, commander, leader, master.

Amirul-Mumineen: leader of the believers, the Caliph

Ard: all things held in honour: women, family, dignity etc.

Bidah: innovation in religion, any act or practice not found in the Sunnah of the Prophet (SAWS) or the Quran.

Dawah: preaching, inviting, propagating, calling (to Islam, Jihad, etc.)

Dai: propagator, one who performs Dawah.

Faraid: compulsory, obligatory duties; plural of Fard.

Fard: compulsory, obligatory duty.

Fard Ain: greatest degree of obligation, compulsory on every Muslim, such as five daily prayers, Hajj, fasting the month of Ramadan and so on.

Fard Kifayah: Initially compulsory, but voluntary upon fulfillment of specific conditions, e.g. Funeral Prayer.

Fatawa: legal rulings, plural of fatwa.

Fatwa: legal ruling.

Fiqh: Islamic jurisprudence.

Fitnah: trial, tribulation, temptation, mischief, strife.

Hadith: report of the Prophet's (SAWS) words or actions.

Hafiz: one who has committed the Quran in its entirety to memory.

Haram: forbidden according to the Shariah.

Hasan: good: second highest degree of authenticity in hadith classification, after Saheeh.

87

Hijaz: the entire Arabian Peninsula, comprising modern-day Saudi Arabia, Kuwait, Qatar, UAE, Bahrain, Oman and Yemen.

Hijrah: emigration in the cause of Allah.

Ijma: consensus of the Ulama (scholars).

Iman: belief, faith and action linked to this.

Jamah: group, gathering, community.

Jizya: head tax imposed by Islam on non-Muslims living under the protection of an Islamic State.

Kafir: disbeliever, infidel, non-Muslim, anyone who does not believe in the creed of Islam.

Kuffar: plural of *Kafir.*

Kufr: disbelief, infidelity, heresy.

Marfu: uninterrupted chain of narration leading to the Prophet (SAWS), therefore reporting directly.

Mathhab: school of thought in Islamic jurisprudence, the four major ones being: Hanafi, Maliki, Shafi and Hanbali.

Muhaditheen: Scholars specialising in *hadith.*

Mushrikun: polytheists, pagans, idolaters, people who practice *Shirk.*

Qiyas: (Principle of *fiqh*) Juristic reasoning, inference by deduction, by analogy.

Rakah: unit of prayer, consisting of one series of prostrations.

Ribat: waiting in preparation to meet the enemy, guarding the frontiers, etc.

Saheeh: correct, certified: highest ranking of authenticity in *hadith* classification.

Salaf: Pious Predecessors: pious people of the first three generations of Islam.

Shariah: Islamic law.

Shaheed: Martyr in the cause of Allah.

Shaytan: Satan.

Sheikh: elder; title usually attributed to man of knowledge.

Shirk: associating partners with Allah, the worship of false gods or idols.

Shuhada: plural of *Shaheed.*

Sunnah: legal ways, practices, orders, acts of worship and statements etc. of the Prophet (SAWS) that are a model followed by Muslims.

Tabligh: to convey, notify, inform, declare.

Tafseer: commentary, explanation, exegesis, interpretation of Quran.

Taqwa: fear or consciousness of Allah, piety, devoutness, religiousness

Ulama: scholars, plural of *Alim*.
Ummah: the entire community of Muslims.
Zakah: compulsory tax of 2.5% per annum paid by Muslims.

APPENDIX E:
EXCERPTS FROM THE WORDS OF SHEIKH ABDULLAH AZZAM

Praise be to Allah, Lord of the Universe and Peace and Blessings be upon the Leader of the Prophets and the Commander of the Mujahideen: Muhammad (SAWS) and upon His Family, His Companions and whoever pursues their method, follows their way and wages Jihad until the Day of Judgement.

Indeed nations are only brought to life by their beliefs and their concepts and they die only with their desires and their lusts. The extent to which righteous convictions and correct beliefs spread within a nation, is the extent to which it plants its roots in the depths of the Earth and sends forth orchards of trunks with their flourishing leaves so that Man can take shade by it from the troubles of life, its financial fever and from the flame of hatred, envy and competition for cheap thrills and temporary enjoyment. As for the Muslim Ummah, it does continue to exist in the course of history of humankind, except by a divine ideology and the blood which flows as a result of spreading this divine ideology and implanting it into the real World.

The life of the Muslim Ummah is solely dependent on the ink of its scholars and the blood of its martyrs. What is more beautiful than the writing of the Ummah's history with both the ink of a scholar and his blood, such that the map of Islamic history becomes coloured with two lines: one of them black, and that is what the scholar wrote with the ink of his pen; and the other one red, and that is what the martyr wrote with his blood. And something more beautiful than this is when the blood is one and the pen is one, so that the hand of the scholar which expends the ink and moves the pen, is the same as the hand which expends its blood and moves the Ummah. The extent to which the number of martyred scholars increases is the extent to which nations are delivered from their slumber, rescued from their decline and awoken from their sleep.

History does not write its lines except with blood. Glory does not build its loft edifice except with skulls. Honour and respect cannot be

90

established except on a foundation of cripples and corpses. Empires, distinguished peoples, states and societies cannot be established except with examples. Indeed those who think that they can change reality, or change societies, without blood, sacrifices and invalids, without pure, innocent souls, then they do not understand the essence of this Deen and they do not know the method of the best of the Messengers (may Allah bless him and grant him peace).

As for those who build nations, they are few in number. Sometimes the Ummah can be built by a single individual who makes a stand by means of which Allah rescues this Deen, just like Abu Bakr (RA) made a stand on the Day of Apostasy; and the day when Imam Ahmad bin Hanbal made a stand when the entire World was speechless at the innovation that the Quran had been created, so Allah saved the Ummah with him.

A small group: they are the ones who carry convictions and ambitions. And an even smaller group from this small group, are the ones who flee from the worldly life in order to spread and act upon these ambitions. And an even smaller group from this elite group, are the ones who sacrifice their souls and their blood in order to bring victory to these ambitions and principles. So, they are the cream of the cream of the cream. It is not possible to reach glory except by traversing this Path. It is not possible for the structures of this Deen to be established, nor for its banner to be raised, nor for its vessel to be launched, except by traversing this Path. This Path is one. In fact, there is no Paradise without this Path:

"Do you really think that you will enter Paradise, before Allah has decided from amongst you, those who fight in His Way and those who are patient?" [Quran 3:142]

Thus the founders of nations and the architects of glories are few. As for the one who wants to architecture glory, then he must be prepared to ascend to the price of glory upon seas of his blood and his sweat, and the blood of those around him and upon the disabilities of those under his authority, until he reaches the price of glory. And glory cannot be architectured except by traversing this Path: the Path of the Blessed Jihad.

Indeed, the manuscripts of history are not scribed except with the blood of these martyrs, except with the stories of these martyrs, except with the examples of these martyrs. By the likes of these martyrs, nations are established, convictions are brought to life and ideologies are made victorious.

And it might seem to the short-sighted eye and narrow mind, and to the individual besieged within the bounds of era and location, that it is a story that happened and finished. The mouth of death opened its mouth, swallowed these martyrs and passed them with its wheel that saves neither old nor young.

However, the clear-sighted eye and the enlightened heart knows that these sacrifices are the provisions of future generations for distant civilisations to come. These stories, these sacrifices and these examples will remain as supercilious signposts upon the entire journey of this Deen, for he who wishes to make this journey from those wayfarers, or follow in the footsteps of this righteous elite

> *" All these are the ones Allah has guided, so follow their guidance ... "*

(Quran 6:90)

Indeed these exemplary individuals from the martyrs broke free from the shackles and fetters of this matter to reach opulence and bliss, and they came to the land of Afghanistan, living in the mountains of Afghanistan, until Allah(swt) honoured them with martyrdom.

So, O' people of ambitions and O' carriers of dawah, do not be miserly with your blood as regards to this Deen. If you really are serious and sincere, then place your blood and souls before the Lord of the Worlds who granted them to you in the first place and then purchased them from you:

"Indeed Allah has purchased from the believers their lives and their possessions in return for Paradise. They fight in the Way of Allah, they kill and are killed ..."
(Quran 9:111)

O' Youths ! O' sons of Islam ! what will cleanse our sins ? What will purify our mistakes ? And what will clean our dirt ? It will not be washed except with the blood of martyrdom, and know that there is no path except this Path. If not, then the Accountability will be difficult, the Scale awaits, The Bridge is ready and your time is running out, so consider it...

Extracts from the lectures of Sheikh Abdullah Azzam titled : ' Will of the Shaheed ' and ' A Message from the Shaheed Sheikh to the Scholars